DUXFORD
AIR SHOWS
50

50 Years of Duxford Air Shows

Published by IWM, Lambeth Road, London SE1 6HZ
iwm.org.uk

ISBN 978-1-912423-63-7

A catalogue record for this book is available from the British Library.
Editorial content by Lara Bateman and Ben Dunnell

Every effort has been made to contact all copyright holders. The
publishers will be glad to make good in future editions any error or
omissions brought to their attention.

Special thanks to Matt Rose, Jack McCarthy, Phil Chaplin and
the Visual Resources team for all of their help with sourcing IWM
images for this publication.

DUXFORD
AIR SHOWS

50

50 Years of Duxford Air Shows

CONTENTS

This page Wrapped up on a surprisingly cold June weekend, visitors to Silver Jubilee Duxford '77 enjoy the display by B-17G *Sally B*. © IWM MH 22667

FOREWORD

Since 1973 IWM Duxford's annual air shows have entertained generations of families and aviation enthusiasts. It is a real pleasure to look back at so many memories of Duxford air shows in this 50th anniversary year. Duxford has always been the place to celebrate our historic past, hosting air show tributes to wartime milestones and the wonderful historic aircraft, many of which call Duxford home. On behalf of the Imperial War Museums and all of our visitors, I would like to thank all the people who over 50 years have contributed so much to the air shows at Duxford, from pilots to those who commentate on the shows or those who serve you a cup of tea! In these pages, we get the chance to look back at the faces, events, aircraft and displays that have created Duxford's air show legacy as one of the UK's leading aviation venues and have set the standard for its current high-quality shows. From Douglas Bader's famous opening of the 1976 show and the appearances of Concorde during the 1980s to Christian Moullec's weird and wonderful display of geese flying alongside a microlight, join us as we chart Duxford's rich air show history across five decades.

There have been so many highlights and there are so many great memories. We hope by telling the stories of 50 years of Duxford air shows, it will inspire you to recall your own golden moments, and I look forward to us experiencing many more into the future.

Caro Howell MBE, Director-General

INTRODUCTION

The history of flying displays in the United Kingdom dates back to October 1909, when the country witnessed its first ever aviation meeting. Staged at Doncaster racecourse, it involved a series of contests between some of the era's pioneer aviators, providing the public with an early chance to see a range of new-fangled flying machines in action. What a trend it set. Today's air shows are among the UK's largest outdoor events, attracting several million spectators per annum. And in this Duxford has long been exceptionally prominent.

During the airfield's time as an active Royal Air Force station, from 1918 to 1961, it was no stranger to large-scale public displays. Most famously, on 6 July 1935 it staged the flypast element of King George V's Jubilee Review of the RAF, the monarch's ground inspection of the aircraft involved having taken place at nearby Mildenhall earlier the same day. A total of 182 aeroplanes, all biplanes, flew past as His Majesty took the salute. On a smaller scale, RAF Duxford was among the stations around the country which played host to Empire Air Days before the war, and Battle of Britain 'At Home' Days after it. Through these very popular occasions the progression of the flying service's capabilities could be seen at close quarters. Given this heritage, it was hugely apposite that, when the Imperial War Museum began using the disused airfield as a large

A view from the air of RAF Duxford's 1937 Empire Air Day. The aircraft nearest the camera, in front of the crowd, are Avro Tutors belonging to the resident Cambridge University Air Squadron. Between the hangars is parked a visiting Handley Page Heyford, while beyond the crowd area are Gloster Gauntlets of No. 19 Squadron, the frontline unit that spent longest stationed at Duxford. © IWM

object store in the early 1970s, the decision was taken to revive Duxford's old air show traditions. Organised by IWM in conjunction with the East Anglian Aviation Society, the Cambridge University Gliding Club and the Shuttleworth Collection, the inaugural Duxford Air Day of a new era took place on 14 October 1973. A significant success – not least as the first time Duxford as a museum site was opened to the public – it paved the way for much, much more. That's the story told by the words and photographs inside this 50th anniversary souvenir publication.

Many air show venues have come and gone over the past half-century. Duxford has been a constant, yet always seeking to do something new. The range of events it's staged, and the display items it's put on, are testament to that. Throughout these endeavours IWM has enjoyed the unique, outstanding support of its onsite partners, without whom much of this 50-year air show history would never have been possible. The contribution of the Duxford Aviation Society continues to be second to none. The likes of The Fighter Collection, the Old Flying Machine Company, Aircraft Restoration Company, Historic Aircraft Collection, B-17 Preservation, Plane Sailing, Anglia Aircraft Restorations/Fighter Aviation Engineering and a host of private owners have made Duxford the scene of standard-setting, epoch-making

Under a quite beautiful rainbow, massed Spitfires make their way out to Duxford's grass and hard runways, ready for the finale of the 2022 Battle of Britain Air Show. © IWM 2022 053 149

warbird displays. And this is to say nothing of everyone who's toiled behind the scenes so it can all happen – an army (air force?) of individuals who may go somewhat unsung, but certainly not unappreciated.

Over the following pages, we take you on a year-by-year journey from 1973 to the present day, charting the development of Duxford air shows and their array of highlights. Memories from organisers, aircraft operators and pilots loom large – and so do some of your own, thanks to the responses we received from air show visitors to our request for recollections.

While the exact make-up of IWM Duxford's calendar has changed with the passage of time, 2023's anniversary season involves more flying displays than at almost any time hitherto. Backing up the main Summer Air Show and Battle of Britain Air Show are several themed Flying Days, the recently introduced Flying Evening and, to close things out, the Flying Finale, which this year takes place on 14 October – exactly 50 years since that initial Air Day under the museum's auspices. In that context, a snapshot of what we enjoyed in 2022 can be used to demonstrate what makes Duxford special. Where else could one witness sixteen Spitfires and four Hurricanes in a mass flypast? How many other civilian shows in Britain can do as the Battle of Britain Air Show did and attract Czech Air Force participation, with Mil Mi-35 and

Uniformed re-enactors add a touch of period flavour on the ground. © IWM 2022 055 0002

Mi-171 battlefield helicopters, or match October's Flying Finale and pull in the Swiss Air Force's Patrouille Suisse aerobatic team of F-5E Tiger IIs? Involvement from the air arms of both countries was new to a Duxford display; indeed, the Czechs were returning to the airfield for the first time since Czechoslovak airmen were stationed there from 1940–1941.

Such potent links between then and now are part of Duxford's particular draw. Few of the types featured in that 1935 Royal Review are still on hand today, but, thanks to the resident Historic Aircraft Collection, the sole airworthy Hawker Fury biplane fighter is an exception. The last pre-war Empire Air Day introduced No. 19 Squadron's new Spitfire Is; now, three such machines regularly take to the skies, along with a host of other 'Spit' marks. Much about the airfield has altered, but take the merest glance at archive photographs or footage showing the view to the south, and it's instantly recognisable. Think of that as you watch, say, a Hurricane, a Spitfire, a Gladiator or a Blenheim dipping its wing while flying along the ridge-line. It renders those images yet more powerful. And, unquestionably, it's why Duxford will always possess its distinct magic.

by Ben Dunnell

The Swiss Air Force's Patrouille Suisse aerobatic team, flying F-5E Tiger II fighters, made its Duxford debut at the Flying Finale in October 2022 – an excellent example of the overseas military support the venue can attract. © Ben Dunnell

DUXFO
VINTAG
DUXFORD AEROD

A day of intensive activity both on the ground and in the air presented by **The Duxford Aviation Society**

Featuring over 80 vehicles representing the Veteran Car Club of Gt.
The 39/45 Vehicle Group and the Duxford Military Vehicle Collecti
In addition at least **100 aircraft** on display including **CONCORDE O**

The flying programme is extensive and will include the Red Arrows, S
Hurricane, Tiger Moth, Gladiator and many others.

Gates open 10·00-19·00   cars £3·00 (including occupants) pedestri

SUNDAY20JUNE19

Presentation in association with the IMPERIAL WAR MUSEUM, the St
TRUST and the CAMBRIDGE UNIVERSITY GLIDING CLUB.

sponsored by
CIBA-GEIGY
the makers of
ARALDITE® and REDUX®
adhesives and resins
for aircraft past, pres

1970s

Duxford's Inaugural Decade

DUXFORD'S GOLDEN MOMENTS: 1970s

Beginning with a single event in 1973, Duxford's air shows quickly became a permanent fixture in the calendar. Joining forces with the East Anglian Aviation Society (EAAS), the Shuttleworth Collection and Cambridge University Gliding Club, IWM opened Duxford airfield to the public for the first time since the museum started using it as a large object store, inviting attendees to see the world's aviation legends first-hand and be immersed in Duxford's rich history.

The **1973** show's flying display was primarily formed of both historic and modern RAF aircraft, including the Gemini Pair team of Jet Provosts, the Battle of Britain Memorial Flight (BBMF), a Hawker Hunter, an English Electric Canberra, a Lockheed C-130 Hercules and a Vickers Varsity. Despite this impressive showcase of Britain's aerial power, the star was IWM's newly restored static P-51D Mustang *Big Beautiful Doll*. It was painted to represent the aircraft of Lieutenant Colonel John D Landers, last commander of the US Army Air Forces' 78th Fighter Group, as a tribute to the special association of the unit with Duxford's historic airfield.

In **1974** air displays were severely restricted in the UK due to a fuel crisis when Saudi Arabia imposed an embargo on oil supplies. However, an open day was held on 23 June at which the EAAS's newly arrived Comet 4 airliner was opened to the public for the first time, attracting a long queue of visitors. A Britannia Airways Boeing 737 was flown in by Captain Mike Russell from Luton Airport to publicise inclusive tour holidays. Coincidentally, its captain was at one time chairman of the EAAS. It was the only 737 ever to land at Duxford, but civil airliners were to become a permanent fixture at the airfield.

The success of the 1974 open day led to a major two-day show in **1975**, with a spectacular line-up of six Spitfires courtesy of the BBMF, Rolls-Royce, Shuttleworth, Adrian Swire, Patrick Lindsay and John Fairey. The Shuttleworth Spitfire, LFVc AR501, was restored at Duxford and made its debut. It was a unique sight for the era and initiated Duxford's long association with

Right Group Captain Sir Douglas Bader shortly after he had inaugurated the Duxford Vintage Day in June 1976. © IWM MH 21182

By 1977 Duxford's air shows had become major aviation events, and the Silver Jubilee Duxford '77 show rose to the occasion with the debut of the first flying Mustang seen in the UK for eight years.

airworthy Spitfires. A notable moment of the show was the first display of B-17G *Sally B* at its new home base, which has become a much-loved and permanent veteran of Duxford. It has graced air shows here with both static and flying displays ever since. International military involvement was added, too, the French Air Force Patrouille de France team of Fouga Magisters proving a major draw.

From **1976** the air shows were to be organised alternately by IWM and the newly formed Duxford Aviation Society (DAS), which took over from the EAAS. The first show organised by the society – the Duxford Vintage Day – was officially opened by the legendary Sir Douglas Bader who flew in with

his Beech Travel Air. The DAS Military Vehicle Wing (MVW) also displayed its vehicles and guns in a grand cavalcade. Public enthusiasm for this item was such that the MVW established its own annual Military Vehicle Show, which became a popular fixture in the Duxford calendar until 2015.

By **1977** Duxford's air shows had become major aviation events, and the Silver Jubilee Duxford '77 show rose to the occasion with the debut of the first flying Mustang seen in the UK for eight years, namely P-51D N5747 of the California-based Mustang Pilots Club. The trans-Atlantic beauty was flown by Tony Ostermeier and undertook a display with *Sally B*, piloted by Don Bullock. The year also, sadly,

marked the last appearances of Ormond Haydon-Baillie's CT-133 Silver Star and Sea Fury before the owner's death.

Come the **1978** season, visitors to the next show organised by the DAS, Duxford '78, were greeted by Concorde 101, which had arrived to join the society's airliner collection and would be open to the public. It had flown in the previous August, only two days before Duxford's runway was shortened, which would have made the landing impossible! Most of the 30 aircraft in the flying programme were of the vintage propeller-driven variety and included Tony Haig-Thomas's remarkable collection of six different examples of the de Havilland Moth

family, which were temporarily based at Duxford at the time.

The final show of Duxford's inaugural decade, in **1979**, celebrated 75 years of Rolls-Royce with a parade of 150 vintage vehicles from the acclaimed manufacturer and a dazzling flying display containing many Rolls-Royce-powered types. Shuttleworth's Bristol F2B Fighter also marked 60 years since Duxford saw its first 'Brisfits' with No. 8 Squadron, RAF. The show finished with an impressive commercial display from a Saudia TriStar.

THE FIRST OF MANY
Duxford Air Day 1973

The first Duxford Air Day took place on Sunday 14 October 1973. It was a cold and dismal day, and few of the visitors to the event could have foreseen that it would turn out to be the first of many Duxford air shows.

The booklet and programme produced for that very first air show 50 years ago differ markedly from the glossy full-colour brochures on offer today. As with all printed ephemera, the style and content reflected society at the time; it now seems pleasantly nostalgic.

A full-colour photograph of IWM's static North American P-51D Mustang *Big Beautiful Doll* parked on the Duxford tarmac adorned the front cover of the 36-page 'Official Souvenir Booklet'. In the absence of an airworthy P-51 in the UK, it was probably considered Duxford's star exhibit.

The introduction written by IWM's Deputy Director Dr Christopher Roads presciently summed up what he believed Duxford ought to represent in the future, by providing an attraction 'both for the recreation of an enthusiastic minority and the enjoyment and recreation of the majority in the community'.

An article titled 'Duxford in the past' was followed by a brief summary headed 'Duxford now', the latter reflecting the uncertainty that still surrounded the future of the airfield in 1973. While Cambridgeshire and Isle of Ely County Council welcomed the Air Day, hoping it would help to guide the authorities towards a plan for Duxford that would 'provide enjoyment for a very large number of people in the future', the council also warned that planning permission to display historic aircraft at the site was only on a temporary basis. Alternative plans were made for Duxford's future use as a country park.

The brochure also contained articles by the organisations responsible for the air show. A piece on IWM's collection of aircraft noted that the museum's exhibits had now 'virtually filled the westernmost hangar at Duxford' and included the newly arrived Avro Shackleton, an English Electric Canberra and the prototype of the Beagle Pup. The latter has recently been made airworthy again.

The East Anglian Aviation Society mentioned the renovation work it had to

DUXFORD

Clockwise Air crew briefing by Flight Lieutenant Les Dawson, Air Traffic Controller. © IWM MH 17802; The cover of the first souvenir programme. © IWM; A glimpse of the crowd attending the first air show. A lot of work had been put in by IWM staff and EAAS volunteers to make the site presentable again, though there were a few 'rough edges'. © IWM MH 17872

undertake on one of the hangars before it could be used and included a photograph of its DC-3 under restoration. Regarding the work the society was undertaking on IWM's collection, it believed 'the greatest success so far is the completely refurbished P-51 Mustang'.

The Shuttleworth Collection stressed the goals it shared with the activities at Duxford. Having given a temporary home to IWM's Sea Venom, which was now back at Duxford, the collection had loaned its own Spitfire V and Avro Anson to Duxford in return; they were being restored by the combined efforts of the Shuttleworth and EAAS engineers.

Gliding operations at Duxford, reported the Cambridge University Gliding Club, were mainly concerned with training to solo standard in a side-by-side open-cockpit glider named *Bluebell*.

CIBA-GEIGY's article reiterated the company's long association with aviation and noted that the 100 dummy aircraft blown up in the *Battle of Britain* film had been made 'using a CIBA-GEIGY adhesive'. The company was a strong early supporter of air shows at the venue; it was based at what is now the Hexcel site on the edge of Duxford village.

The 12-page programme of events was printed in black and white on a yellowish-beige stock. The reason a separate listing of the flying elements and timings was needed was because they were subject to change and had to be printed after the main brochure had gone to press. Much the same thing still happens today.

A disclaimer warned visitors that because the airfield buildings were now 55 years old and had been largely disused for the last dozen years, 'their condition is not all it might be', and reminded patrons, 'you enter the airfield at your own risk'.

The activities on offer before the flying began included an exhibition by CIBA-GEIGY and a chance to see the 35-year-old Miles Magister under restoration by the EAAS, an aeroplane which flies today in private hands from Old Warden. There was also an opportunity to sit in the cockpit section of an unspecified 'modern RAF jet', which turned out to be a Hawker Hunter, and if that did not appeal visitors could watch a one-hour film programme courtesy of the IWM Film Archive.

Pleasure flights were available, much as they are today. 'For a small charge' visitors could see Duxford from the air in a Britten-Norman Islander belonging to Humber Airways.

Static aeroplanes were on display in one of the hangars and out on the tarmac, including the prototype Beagle 206, a Fairey Gannet, a Junkers Ju 52/3m (really a French-built Amiot AAC1) and 'several aircraft kindly made available by their owners'.

Adding to the aircraft on show were several visitors that flew in for the day. A Royal Navy de Havilland Sea Devon, an RAF Westland Whirlwind HAR10 and a Gloster Javelin FAW9, XH897, from the Aeroplane and Armament Experimental Establishment turned up. The Javelin was retired a couple of years later: its final flight was into Duxford to join the IWM collection.

Civilian visitors were mainly light aircraft, among them being three Druine Turbulents, two Tiger Moths, two Austers, a Stampe, a de Havilland Chipmunk and a Piper Cherokee. There was a relatively rare French-built Wassmer WA41 Super Baladou, which acted as an airborne camera-ship, and a much larger Hawker Siddeley HS748 twin-turboprop airliner used by the Civil Aviation Flying Unit.

Ten minutes before the flying display was due to begin, the national anthem was played. As there is no mention of a band being present, this was presumably a recording relayed over the loudspeakers. The anthem was followed by an opening address by one of the most charismatic leaders the RAF has ever had: Air Chief Marshal Sir Harry Broadhurst GCB KBE DSO DFC AFC.

'Broady', as he was known, had a long and distinguished career in the RAF. Stationed at Duxford with No. 19 Squadron between the wars, during 1940 he saw action at the Battle of France and the Battle of Britain, and in 1941 he led the Hornchurch-based Spitfires on sweeps over France. His final tally as a fighter pilot was 13 enemy aircraft destroyed. Promoted to Air Vice-Marshal, Broadhurst took command of the Desert Air Force in 1943 and laid down the principles of how aircraft should be used to support the Army. He commanded No. 83 Group of the 2nd Tactical Air Force during the D-Day landings and beyond. In the post-war years he was Commander-in-Chief of Bomber Command, retiring as an Air Chief Marshal in 1957.

The air display began at two o'clock, as always with the proviso that it was subject to weather conditions and serviceability. Appearing first were the RAF's Lancaster, together with the Spitfire and Hurricane of the Battle of Britain Flight, which the Lancaster was soon to formally join. The RAF also displayed an English Electric Canberra B2, a Gloster Meteor F8, a Lockheed Hercules C1, a Vickers Varsity T1 and a Hawker Hunter F6, together with the BAC Jet Provost T5s of No. 3 Flying Training School's Gemini Pair aerobatic team.

The Shuttleworth Collection's contribution to the flying display comprised a Hunting Percival Provost, the Avro Tutor and Miles Magister; its Gloster Gladiator was programmed to attend, but does not seem to have done so. Hawker Siddeley brought its de Havilland Mosquito, the Civil Aviation Flying Unit at Stansted supplied a de Havilland Dove, and Hunting Surveys contributed a Douglas DC-3. The Turbulents of the Tiger Club, air display stalwarts to this day, added their own brand of aerial entertainment.

The Royal Navy displayed its Historic Flight's Fairey Swordfish, Hawker Sea Fury and Fairey Firefly, along with a Westland Wasp helicopter; the Army Air Corps demonstrated two Westland Scouts. There was also an exhibition of aerobatic gliding by the Cambridge University Gliding Club.

The final item of the day was the lift-off from the display arena of *Aquarius*, an orange and yellow hot-air balloon piloted by former European record holder Dr John Gore.

A little over an hour later Duxford closed its gates. Nobody knew then what would happen to the airfield in the future, or whether there would ever be another air display there. Yet from such humble and uncertain beginnings sprang the 50 years of IWM Duxford air shows we are celebrating today. Duxford has indeed more than fulfilled the desire of IWM's Deputy Director Dr Christopher Roads that it should become a place containing 'a living collection of aircraft', with 'a body of enthusiastic and able volunteers for its maintenance and restoration, and a serviceable runway.'

TIMETABLE OF MAIN EVENTS

11.00 Programme of continuous attractions opens
Static Displays and Exhibitions, Pleasure Flights, Film Show etc.

12.15 RAF Police Dog Display in the Arena

1.15 Display by C Squadron, 21st SAS (Artists) Regiment (V) in front
of the Public Enclosure

1.50 National Anthem
Opening Address
by Air Chief Marshal Sir Harry Broadhurst GCB KBE DSO DFC AFC

2.00 Flying Display
Subject to weather conditions and operational requirements, the Flying
Display is expected to include the following elements:
AVRO LANCASTER (RAF)
SUPERMARINE SPITFIRE & HAWKER HURRICANE (RAF)
ENGLISH ELECTRIC/BAC CANBERRA (RAF)
HUNTING PERCIVAL PROVOST (Shuttleworth Collection)
LOCKHEED HERCULES (RAF)
AVRO TUTOR & MILES MAGISTER (Shuttleworth Collection)
DE HAVILLAND DOVE (CAFU Stansted)
DOUGLAS DAKOTA
HAWKER HUNTER (RAF)
GLOSTER GLADIATOR (Shuttleworth Collection)
VICKERS VARSITY (RAF)
FAIREY SWORDFISH, HAWKER SEA FURY, FAIREY FIREFLY (RNAS
Yeovilton)
DE HAVILLAND MOSQUITO (Hawker Siddeley, Hatfield)
AEROBATIC GLIDING by the Cambridge University Gliding Club
WESTLAND SCOUT Helicopter Handling Demonstration by the Army
Air Corps
WESTLAND WASP Helicopter Winching Demonstration by the Fleet
Air Arm

4.30 Hot-Air Balloon Ascent
by Dr John Gore in 'Aquarius' from the Arena

4.45 RAF Police Dog Display in the Arena

6.00 Airfield closes

Introduction

by

DR. CHRISTOPHER ROADS.

Deputy Director of the Imperial War Museum and

Chairman of the Duxford Air Day Planning & Management Committee.

The RAF Station at Duxford, like the Royal Air Force itself, came into existence in the last year of the Great War, and remained until 1961 in the forefront of the Service's activities, forty-three years of distinguished involvement in the aerial history of Great Britain. That involvement, which is outlined elsewhere in this booklet, has established a tradition of which the four bodies, the Imperial War Museum, the East Anglian Aviation Society, the Cambridge University Gliding Club and the Shuttleworth Collection, currently active at Duxford and cooperating in the organisation of the Air Day are deeply aware.

Those of us who live in Cambridgeshire and many living further afield, feel in the name of 'Duxford' a distinct nostalgia for the period when, although under the shadow of enemy invasion, there was evident the most remarkable bond of comradeship and common purpose in the community. We hope that in some small measure the Air Day will bring into the context of the future use and development of RAF Duxford the same spirit of mutual cooperation for the benefit of all in the community.

Nothing surely can be more appropriate in the setting of this historic airfield than that there continues to be there indefinitely into the future a living collection of aircraft reflecting on broad lines, and within obvious limitations, the history of aerial warfare in this century. A living collection requires, inter alia, a body of enthusiastic and able volunteers for its maintenance and restoration, and a serviceable runway. Both now exist, as the Air Day vividly demonstrates : there is no doubt that the first will continue to flourish and expand so there must equally be no possibility that the second either deteriorates or is lost. This way Duxford will, in the fullest sense, provide both for the recreation of an enthusiastic minority and the enjoyment and recreation of the majority in the community.

Duxford is also an experiment, and a most successful one, in partnership between an official body and an unofficial one, between the public and private sectors, between a national museum and a local volunteer group. It demonstrates how considerable and how important are the benefits both ways thus engendered, opening, as it dramatically does, wider vistas for both museum and society as well as for city dweller and countryman, professional man and manual worker. Duxford could be almost as important a blazon on the road into the future as it is in our recent past.

SALLY B

A proud lady

by Ben Dunnell

Duxford had hosted just one air show when, on 16 March 1975, an unpainted Boeing B-17G Flying Fortress swept in over the airfield, beating up the taxiway and passing low — very low — in front of the control tower.

The museum wasn't yet open to the public on a regular basis, but a small crowd of the resident volunteers and gliding club members still turned out to watch the occasion, some getting an especially good view from the top of the tower as the American bomber flew by. After a few more passes, it landed and taxied in to park, immediately being surrounded by curious onlookers. The aircraft wore no markings other than the US registration, N17TE, crudely applied over its previous French identity which was still carried atop its wings, and the name Euroworld on the nose.

Nearly five decades and countless Duxford displays later, this very aeroplane is still there. It looks rather different, but its attraction has never diminished. Indeed, *Sally B*, as the B-17 has been named for almost all that time, is arguably now more important than ever. No other Flying Fortress remains airworthy in Europe, and as the number of surviving veterans diminishes, it acts as an increasingly powerful flying memorial to the thousands of Americans who paid the ultimate price for victory in Europe during the Second World War. Given Duxford's own US Eighth Air Force history, *Sally B*'s appearances at its own base take on a particular potency.

Left Andrew Dixon and Peter Kuypers displaying B-17G *Sally B* at the 2010 Autumn Air Show, which celebrated the aircraft's 65th birthday. © David Halford

Let's rewind to 1975. Euroworld, the name on the aircraft when it flew in, was the company which acquired it from France's Institut Géographique National, operator of several B-17Gs for aerial survey and mapping work. Established by Don Bullock and Ted White, aircraft ferrying was Euroworld's business, and it intended to sell the Fortress on. But by the time of the Biggin Hill Air Fair, scene of its public display debut in mid-May, White had christened the machine *Sally B*, after his Danish-born partner Elly Sallingboe, with accompanying nose art. In newly applied US Army Air Force markings, it made a splendid sight.

A few weeks later there came Duxford '75, the first chance for the B-17 to display on its new home turf. In a show packed with star acts, it was a major highlight. So began a run of participation that's seen *Sally B* fly at the majority of Duxford displays ever since. In those days, there weren't the myriad opportunities that exist now to team the Fortress with suitable escort fighters, but one arose at Duxford '77 when the P-51D belonging to the Mustang Pilots' Club came over for a visit from Van Nuys, California. A historical pairing not witnessed for many years was the result.

It was in 1979 that Ted White established B-17 Preservation to operate the aircraft, but tragedy was not far away. He and his colleague Mark Campbell were killed in June 1982 when Ted's North American Harvard crashed in Malta. Despite her devastation, Elly Sallingboe decided there was only one thing to do: carry on. The cowling of *Sally B*'s starboard inner engine was painted in a black-and-yellow chequered pattern in tribute to Ted, whose Harvard had carried the same markings. Even then, campaigning a four-engined heavy bomber in private hands was a pricey business, but, Elly told the author, 'Let's put it this way – I was young, the team was young, we just wanted to do it and we would find a way.'

That ethos has persisted. To raise awareness and some funds, Elly and a large team of volunteers organised Britain's first dedicated warbird air show, the Great Warbirds Air Display, at West Malling during 1982. When the Kent airfield was turned into a housing estate after the 1991 edition, Great Warbirds moved to Wroughton in Wiltshire, running there until 1994. It had blazed a trail, and unquestionably influenced Duxford events to come.

So it was the case that, as the 1990s and 2000s wore on, *Sally B* generally flew with at least one American fighter in every Duxford show. The Autumn Air Show of 2010 was dedicated to the B-17, marking the type's own 75th anniversary and *Sally B*'s 65th; it opened proceedings with an escort of three P-51s, and a pair of US Air Force F-15C Eagles a little way behind. The following year, the aircraft uniquely had its own date on the Duxford calendar, the one-off *Sally B* and Friends Day, conjuring up the old Great Warbirds spirit on a smaller scale and featuring a variety of mixed formations.

Perhaps best of all, 2015's VE Day Anniversary Air Show saw the B-17 leading the centrepiece Salute Formation. Joining it in close company were three P-51s, provided by The Fighter Collection, the Old Flying Machine Company and the Norwegian Spitfire Foundation, along with TFC's P-40F Warhawk and FM-2 Wildcat. After a short interval came the second element, consisting of Plane Sailing's Catalina, Aces High's C-47A Skytrain and a Beech 18 owned by Phil and Allie Dunnington. Coming as *Sally B* notched up 40 years on the display circuit, it was a double celebration. And still new combinations for the beloved bomber to feature in have been found. A heavy trio with two C-47s premiered at the 2017 Battle of Britain Air Show, all three aircraft flown by *Sally B*'s then roster of captains. Last June's Summer Air Show found the Fortress with the Extra EA300 aerobatic aircraft of the Blades team on its wings.

These spectacles have been remarkable, really. Several times in the past, the B-17 has been laid low by technical problems; on each occasion, it's bounced back. The expense of operating such a machine only increases year on year, but this one, somehow, keeps going. Its dedicated volunteers, and the contributions made by members of the *Sally B* Supporters' Club, have helped see to that. Above all, it's down to the sheer determination of Elly Sallingboe to keep this flying memorial alive. Without her, it would have gone long ago.

The support from IWM in giving the B-17 its base since that grey, windswept day in 1975 has been crucial too, something Elly is always keen to stress. And, in turn, Duxford has great cause to thank her and *Sally B* for some of the highlights of its 50 years of air shows.

To join the *Sally B* Supporters' Club, visit **sallyb.org.uk**

'Let's put it this way – I was young, the team was young, we just wanted to do it and we would find a way.'

Above *Sally B* operator Elly Sallingboe flying on the B-17 between venues in 2014. © Steve Carter;
Below The Salute Formation centrepiece of the VE Day Anniversary Air Show in 2015 was, fittingly, led by B-17G *Sally B* as it notched up four decades on the display circuit. With it were five Duxford-based fighters. © Ben Dunnell

1980s

Boom Time for Duxford

DUXFORD'S GOLDEN MOMENTS: 1980s

The booming 1980s saw Duxford expand its repertoire to multiple annual air shows and commemorations. With the help of new partners, such as the Old Flying Machine Company and The Fighter Collection, and the continued support of Duxford Aviation Society, alongside other private aircraft owners, the events gathered momentum.

They gave rise to the unique displays from commercial aircraft, the military and the mass formations that have long since characterised Duxford's air shows.

The decade began with prominent commercial flypasts at the DAS-organised Duxford '80, the display opening with an Air Bridge Carriers Argosy and a Transmeridian CL-44. In addition to the military aircraft on display, participants included Wing Commander Ken Wallis with his 'James Bond' autogyro, *Little Nellie*. IWM also staged its Battle of Britain 40th Anniversary Display the same year, naturally featuring the BBMF's Hurricane and Spitfire IIa, the latter in No. 19 Squadron markings, while the Shuttleworth and Rolls-Royce Spitfires were the penultimate display. The show also marked the first Duxford appearance by Percival Mew Gull G-AEXF, the famed racer then owned by Martin Barraclough. The Aces High C-47 G-DAKS additionally appeared in 'Ruskin Air Services'

colours for the filming of ITV's *Airline*.

Commercial aircraft were again prominent at Duxford Vintage '81, with a flypast from an Aer Turas Britannia and displays from an AirUK F27 Friendship, Instone Air Line Bristol Freighter and Air Leicester Embraer Bandeirante. Tony Haig-Thomas flew Sandy Topen's newly restored Vampire T11, and the whole of Robs Lamplough's Duxford-based Fighter Wing Display Team – Harvards, Yak-11, Beech D17 and Criquet – appeared for the first time. A prototype of the Edgley Optica gave a surprise demo in the hands of Hugh Field on its way back from the Paris Air Show. The **1981** show also launched the 'Superhangar' project; a USAF A-10A displayed as a Duxford newcomer and was supported by a static USAF HC-130, HH-53 and OV-10.

Described in the *Duxford Aviation Society News* as 'the greatest aerial spectacle at Duxford since the 1935 Jubilee Review', DAS

Right The commentator in action at the Rolls-Royce on Wheel and Wing show in 1984. © IWM DUX/84/5/20

achieved a cherished ambition at the **1982** show with the participation of Concorde at a Duxford air display for the first time; this was thanks to British Airways and a charter company which filled G-BOAB with passengers, all too happy to experience a demonstration during their flight. On retirement by BA, HS Trident 2E G-AVFB performed a short display before landing to join the DAS collection.

In **1983** the Burma Star Association, alongside IWM, staged the Mountbatten Memorial Display in memory of Earl Mountbatten. The USAF displayed an F-15C Eagle for first time at Duxford, while a C-5A Galaxy became the largest aircraft ever to appear at the venue. The 1983 show also welcomed newcomer Lindsey Walton's Corsair.

1984 marked Rolls-Royce's 80th anniversary and was commemorated with the Rolls-Royce on Wheel and Wing show. Many classic Rolls-Royce vehicles and Rolls-Royce-powered aircraft were in attendance. Shuttleworth's 'Brisfit', the oldest aircraft present, was contrasted with the modern-day RAF Hawk and Army Air Corps Lynx aerobatic displays. Additional highlights were superb routines from Ray Hanna in Spitfire MH434 and Stephen Grey in P-51D *Candyman/Moose*, both of which had recently arrived at Duxford. A British Caledonian BAC One-Eleven also displayed, while a British Air Ferries Viscount, an AirUK F27 and an RAF Andover made for a fine gathering of civil and military transports. In dreadful weather at Duxford '84, BA Concorde made two majestic appearances, with 90 passengers on board.

Duxford extended a warm and royal welcome in **1985** to the Queen Mother, who attended the 50th anniversary of King George V's Jubilee Review of the RAF. It was 50 years to the day since the Queen Mother formed part of the Royal party at the Review itself, at which a commemorative flypast was staged; now 'her' Queen's Flight Wessex became the first Royal aircraft ever to land at Duxford. A myriad of mid-1930's aircraft took part in the celebrations, including Tiger Moth, Hind and Gladiator. Aside from the Red Arrows, Vulcan and others, the RAF provided a Battle of Britain Memorial Flight Spitfire XIX/Tornado F2 duo, with the Tornado flown by Rick Peacock-Edwards – the future flying control committee chairman at IWM Duxford.

In **1986** the Old Flying Machine Company (OFMC) collaborated with IWM to stage the first Classic Fighter Display. The show featured the aircraft of the OFMC and The Fighter Collection (TFC) as well as numerous guest aircraft. One highlight was TFC's P-47D Thunderbolt, newly painted as the 78th Fighter Group's *No Guts — No Glory!*, recalling the type's presence in the Second World War. The Duxford '86 show celebrated ten years of the Duxford Aviation Society. While the

weather elsewhere in the UK hindered the programme, the flying items ranged from a CFM Shadow microlight to the Red Arrows and Concorde.

Following the success of the OFMC's 1986 show with IWM, plans were put in place for a unique combination of attractions at the Classic Fighters and Fire Engines season-opener of 1987, but strong winds grounded all flying at the event. The Burma Star Air Day was marred by Russavia's pleasure-flying Dragon Rapide ending up in a car park after a take-off incident.

In **1988** the Spitfire Jubilee Air Show marked 50 years since the type entered service at RAF Duxford; the show gathered 13 examples of the famous warbird and saw most of them taking to the skies. The display also included some unusual routines with a BBMF four-ship, a father-and-son Spitfire duo performed by Ray and Mark Hanna, and a Tiger Moth/Spitfire formation. Among the

many veterans in attendance was former Vickers-Supermarine test pilot Jeffrey Quill, who delivered No. 19 Squadron's first Mk I to RAF Duxford in 1938. The Autumn Air Day saw the last appearance of the red Spitfire XIV G-FIRE before its move to the USA.

The Classic Fighter Display returned in **1989** and was staged collaboratively by both TFC and OFMC. It attracted more than 23,000 spectators. All three of Europe's airworthy Buchóns, from the OFMC, Charles Church and Hans Dittes, flew and were tailchased by three Spitfires, one of which was Charles Church's ill-fated Mk V EE606 making its debut. The finale was a mass flypast of Second World War fighters – the forerunner of the mass 'Balbo' flypasts which were to become such a popular feature of future displays. Bad weather at Duxford '89 prevented many aircraft from participating, but the show saw the first appearance of a Merlin Trio, featuring TFC's Spitfire IX and

P-51D and OFMC's P-51D in an aerobatic routine. It was also, sadly, the last time an RAF Buccaneer would be seen at Duxford. By contrast, the Autumn Air Day brought the debut of TFC's Hurricane XII, a stalwart of the scene ever since.

Above A line-up of nine airworthy Spitfires at the 1988 Spitfire Jubilee show. © Andrew Read; HM Queen Elizabeth The Queen Mother walking to her Wessex helicopter prior to departure from the July 1985 display. Surprisingly, the Queen's Flight Wessex was the first Royal aircraft ever to land at Duxford. © IWM DUX/85/9/26

in conversation with
TED INMAN

Ted Inman, Duxford's former Director between 1978–2004, talks us through the early days of air shows at IWM's famous airfield.

What was your first role at IWM, and how did you become the 'Keeper' of IWM Duxford?

My first role at IWM was as a research assistant in the Department of Documents, with responsibility for the museum's archive of German documents. In this role I volunteered, as did many curators, to help staff at the first Duxford Air Show in October 1973. My task was to collect admission money on one of the gates. My official involvement in Duxford began the following year as assistant to the then Deputy Director-General, supporting him in negotiations with the government and Cambridgeshire County Council to secure the Duxford site for IWM. This led to an increasing curatorial and management involvement in Duxford until I was appointed Keeper in 1978.

What characterised Duxford's air shows in the 1980s, and how did they evolve from the earlier shows of the 1970s?

The main difference was the growing contingent of private operators at Duxford and the extraordinary increase in the quality of their collections (Old Flying Machine Company and The Fighter Collection), and their willingness to contribute and participate in shows as part of the basis on which they kept their aircraft at Duxford. With this participation we had the capacity to put on four shows a year, two more local ones in May and October, and two more ambitious shows, the Classic Fighter Show which later developed into Flying Legends, and the September show, which benefitted both from a continuing high level of RAF participation as in the '70s, and the high-quality input of the 'new' private collections.

...The air shows became 'the icing on the cake'.

This page Mrs Frankland, the wife of Dr Noble Frankland, former IWM Director, and the Keeper of Duxford, Ted Inman (centre), after inspecting the *City of Lincoln* Avro Lancaster at Duxford Air Day in June 1982. © IWM/82/24/46

The other significant change was that for much of the '70s the air shows were the main opportunity for the public to access the museum and its collections. Only towards the end of the '70s was the museum fully open all year round so that the presentation of the whole site and the preservation and display of its collections were the year-round priority, and the air shows became 'the icing on the cake'.

Both contributed to Duxford's growing international reputation which was the basis for the huge steps forward with the American Air Museum in 1997 and AirSpace in 2007.

How did the large scale air shows compare to the smaller shows? What were the challenges of organising them?

The main challenge of the larger shows was how to predict the attendance and manage the traffic; we had some serious reputational issues arising both from traffic jams before the most popular shows and delays in people leaving after them. The smaller ones were more predictable and more relaxed in terms of overall organisation. In both cases, however, the key issues were around flight safety, the coordination and briefing of the show, and monitoring of displays and pilots. I like to think we set very high standards.

Is there anything in retrospect that you would change about the air shows from the period?

Maybe to have held fewer of them – between 1977 and June 2004, I was present at and responsible for all the shows held at Duxford, around 90 in all. But I shouldn't say that – it was a challenging and rewarding part of the job and the source of much public enjoyment.

'I loved the Spitfires and the Red Arrows during the 1980s, but I always remember the tank display (Challenger/ Leopard) running over a car that was flattened without the tank even rising up! What incredible machines.'

David Brierley

YOUR MEMORIES | 1980s

'My first date with my husband, my then boyfriend, was at the September 1985 Duxford air show. We both loved air shows, and he brought me all the way from north London to attend. While we were there, he took a photo of me, and had it developed to keep in his wallet; he carried the photo around in his wallet since the day he took it. We married in 1988 and returned to the September Duxford air show every year without fail to celebrate our first date and Duxford's role in our love story. Over the years we've seen so many wonderful aeroplanes, and particularly recall the Concorde that came over and flew really low at one of the air shows. All so very amazing!'

Yvonne Wyatt

From left A C-5A Galaxy, then Duxford's largest visitor, at the Mountbatten Memorial Display in 1983. © Andrew Read; The museum's Avro Vulcan on display at Duxford's Air Day in June 1982. © IWM 82/24/15; Attendees take shelter under the wings of the ex-British Airways HS Trident 2E G-AVFB during heavy thunderstorms at the Rolls-Royce Wheel and Wing show in June 1984. © IWM DUX/84/5/25; A classic Duxford scene from September 1985: warbirds prominent on the flightline, in the form of Stephen Grey's Bearcat and P-51D, the Royal Navy Historic Flight Firefly and BAe's Mosquito, museum aircraft behind the barriers. © Key Collection

A GLIMPSE BEHIND THE SCENES

Whilst you are enjoying our show today, spare a thought for the team of people who work together to make it all happen and the preparation which starts many months beforehand. Basic necessities (like toilets), have to be ordered to supplement the normal facilities provided on a day-to-day basis at the Museum. Catering and hospitality have to be planned in detail well in advance of the event. Choosing the flying participants is most enjoyable but is always a compromise and it is impossible to please everyone.

As the show day approaches the number of tasks to be completed increases. The small permanent staff of the Museum is supplemented by volunteers and staff hired for the occasion and all of these need to be briefed and supervised. At this stage my role is rather like a puppeteer holding and drawing together a large number of strings. So that on the eve of the show all is ready to go, plans are made, staff prepared, tents up, programme planned, food and drink ordered, barriers up, road signs out, radio and TV briefed and waste bins emptied.

This morning I will have risen early and had a look at the weather before travelling to Duxford to arrive at about 0700. At that time all is usually quiet, the traders erecting their stalls, aircraft being wheeled out and checked, the admissions and shop staff are counting their floats and the car parking team making their final preparations. Such peace does not last.

The moment the public gates are open all the various parts of my job require attention. Most of these numerous tasks are easily dealt with but they are all important as they are the wheels of the machine which is Duxford '89. They range from queries at live-side control to tracking down supplies of soap for the toilets. Or from last minute changes to the flying programme to problems with the PA system. A quick gulp of coffee and suddenly it's lunch time.

Whilst you're relaxing and enjoying your lunch we are making final arrangements for the flying display itself, briefing the pilots and checking the final programme. The ground staff are coping with everything from lost children and electrical

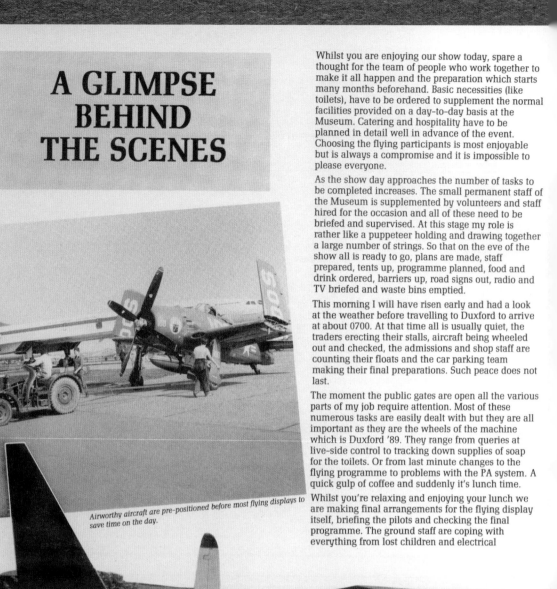

Airworthy aircraft are pre-positioned before most flying displays to save time on the day.

From left to right: Corsair, Mustang and Kingcobra of The Fighter Collection.

breakdowns to cars leaking petrol in the car park. All must be completed before the flying starts as once the display commences such tasks are much more difficult.

Isolated in the Control Tower, the air traffic staff have worked hard this morning bringing in visiting aircraft and participants, all of which have to be found a parking space by our team of volunteer aircraft handlers. Once the show starts I must join the Tower crew as they ensure that the display flying goes according to plan, holding or bringing forward items so that what you see is as continuous a display as we can provide. My day will probably not finish until you are well on your way home as there are many jobs to be completed to restore the Museum to its normal routine.

At the end of it all the object of the exercise is to give you an exciting and entertaining day. If we succeed in that the whole of the Duxford team will feel that all their efforts have been worthwhile.

John Smith, Airfield Manager

Preparations underway for the big day.

Display flying the
P51D Mustang
By Hoof Proudfoot

Photo: M. Shreeve

'Hoof' Proudfoot in the P40 cockpit.

Hoof Proudfoot

Hoof Proudfoot joined the Royal Air Force in 1958 and among the military aircraft he has flown are the Jet Provost, Vampire, Hunter and Harrier. During his RAF career he flew an instructional exchange tour with the US Marine Corps to convert their pilots to the Harrier. Hoof holds the Queens Commendation and Air Force Cross.

Hoof is now a Captain with Britannia Airways and is Chief Pilot for The Fighter Collection which is based at Duxford Airfield.

The American P51D Mustang was arguably the most famous offensive fighter aircraft in the European Theatre of Operations during World War Two. It had the unique capabilities of extremely long range, it could escort the B17 Flying Fortress bomber formations to their targets in Europe and back which sometimes took up to 6 or 7 hours, and it possessed the air combat ability of being equal or better than anything the Germans possessed at that time, other than the jet fighters introduced late in the war. The Mustang was well named after the fiery American wild horse. It is a powerful and agile aircraft which is capable of very high performance, but at the same time it can be unforgiving to the pilot foolish enough not to treat its handling characteristics with respect.

What is it like to fly the Mustang for display purposes? The best way to describe such a flight is to take the reader through a typical display sequence here at Duxford.

START UP & TAKE OFF

Having checked out all the incidentals prior to the actual flight (weather, timing, airfield restrictions etc), I now check out the aircraft itself. I complete a full walk-round inspection and make sure that all is in order and the aircraft has the fuel I require for this short flight of approximately 10 minutes. I put on the parachute, strap in and connect up my helmet. With the battery master switch on, the aircraft comes electrically to life and I carry out a thorough pre-start cockpit check. With approximately 10 mins to go before take off, it is time to start and allow the engine to warm up. I signal for the ground battery trolley to be plugged in (to save the aircraft battery power on start up) and call for 'Clear Propeller' from our ground crew. I am cleared to start from outside and with the magneto switches on I operate the fuel primer intermittently and engage the starter. The Rolls Royce Merlin turns over slowly, swinging round the big metal four bladed propeller – a couple of coughs from the exhaust stacks and the engine bursts into life with a crackling roar. I slide the fuel mixture control into the 'Run' detent, watch the oil pressure rising and adjust the throttle to give between 1000 – 1200 rpm. External power is

removed and the aircraft is back on its own power. A few more checks and then a radio call to Duxford tower for taxy clearance. During the taxy out the view from the cockpit is good – it is restricted forward because of the big engine but it is not as bad as some contemporary fighters.

I arrive at the holding point, short of the runway, and note that the oil and coolant temperatures, which are automatically controlled by their own shutter doors, are sufficient to run up the engine to check that it is operating correctly. After the run up I close the cockpit canopy and ask for take off clearance. When this is given I line up on the runway centre-line and hold the control column hard back to engage the tail-wheel steering lock. A final check that all is okay and I am ready to roll. I release the brakes and slowly increase the power.

Too much power too soon and I will not have the rudder authority to keep straight due to the high engine torque. As the aircraft rapidly accelerates I apply more power up to 61″ of boost, note 3000 rpm, and ease the control column forward to raise the tail and at the same time apply both full right aileron and rudder to counteract the torque. The engine noise is deafening and the acceleration fantastic. I can now see where I am going over the engine cowling and at appropximately 110 mph I lift the aircraft off the ground and retract the wheels. Safely airborne I reduce to climbing power – 46″ of boost and 2700 rpm. The aircraft is still accelerating rapidly and as the speed passes 180 mph I bank around to the right to pass across the A505 road behind Duxford, climbing and accelerating all the time. A quick scan of the instruments shows that all is well with the aircraft and that the automatics controlling the oil and coolant temperatures are doing their job correctly.

THE DISPLAY

I now pass beyond the end of the Duxford runway and turn the corner beyond the M11 to run in at 300 mph at 500 feet up, along the main runway. Wings level and abeam the Control Tower I pull up at 4G (4 times the force of gravity). The Mustang curves up in the first part of a loop and just before reaching the top I see the inverted horizon coming into view. The speed has dropped to about 120 mph and I use a small amount of right rudder to keep straight. The

altimeter shows that the height is safe for me to complete the loop and I pull down the far side of the loop, gaining speed all the time. I hold the aircraft level at the bottom of the loop and accelerate towards the aircraft boundary fence. I pull up once more and pass over the top of the loop, and as the airfield appears inverted in the windscreen I push forward and hold the aircraft in an inverted 45 degree dive for about 1 second. I now apply full aileron and top rudder to roll out and dive down along the runway, heading in the opposite direction. I now repeat the same manoeuvre at the other end of the runway. A quick check that the aircraft is operating satisfactorily as I approach mid-field and bank hard round to complete a full 360 degree turn in front of the tower. This will demonstrate the Mustangs turning performance. I now position for a roll along the runway line.

The speed is approximately 250 mph and I pull the nose up to about 15 degrees above the horizon, hold it there, and apply full aileron. The aircraft completes a rapid roll and I level out and reverse the turn. I repeat the same type of manoeuvre except with a pause at each 90 degrees of roll (a hesitation roll) and re-position for the final low pass and turn to downwind. I run up the runway at about 50 feet and 250 mph and bank hard left and pull up to down-wind, gradually reducing power as I do so. I begin to lower the variable flaps and at 170 mph lower the wheels. I am now half way round the final turn and with 140 mph, full flaps and all checks complete I am set up for landing. I have a good view over the nose and approach the end of the runway at 110 mph. As I get close to the ground I gently round out by applying back pressure on the control column and simultaneously reduce power.

The aircraft settles onto the runway with a slight bump and once firmly down I apply full back control column to lock the tail-wheel steering and use the rudder to keep straight. As the speed drops off I gradually apply the brakes, raise the flaps and manually open the cooling shutter doors to assist the engine to cool down. I open the cockpit canopy and taxy in carefully. Flight time was just over 6 minutes using about 1–1½ gallons of fuel a minute, and although the time was short it has been reasonably demanding and totally satisfying.

Mustangs flew operationally from Duxford during World War Two. It is an honour to fly the aircraft and a privilege to present the Mustang as a flying memorial to the brave fighter crews of that great conflict.

CONCORDES OVER DUXFORD

by Duxford Aviation Society

As an onsite partner of IWM Duxford, Duxford Aviation Society (DAS) exists to preserve and present to the public historic British airliners. Since its formation in 1975 it has assembled the most important collection of post-war British airliners to be seen anywhere.

The 13 airliners of the British Airliner Collection range from an Avro York used in the Berlin Airlift in 1948–1949 to a BAe 146 'Statesman' used by the RAF's 'Royal' squadron from 1986 until its retirement to Duxford in 2022. It owns the world's oldest surviving-turbine powered airliner, as well as the aircraft that made the first scheduled transatlantic crossing by a jet airliner. Some of these aircraft are the only surviving examples and arrived at Duxford by road to be completely rebuilt by DAS volunteers. One of Duxford's most popular exhibits is Concorde 101, donated to DAS by the UK government and flown to Duxford in 1977.

Concorde remains an icon today, and in the 1980s was the high point of any air show and many major public events. In June 1982,

DAS achieved a cherished ambition with the first flying appearance of Concorde at an IWM Duxford air show. At the time British Airways' Concordes were being used by charter companies, and one of them was persuaded to add an excursion to Duxford to one of its charter flights. G-BOAB flew past with passengers on board and gave a 15-minute 'demonstration' – typically displays were not allowed with passengers. However, the fact that the co-pilot was a DAS member may have been a persuading factor! This spectacular display set a precedent for Concorde's appearance at future air shows at Duxford. Also notable at this show was the arrival of the latest addition to the DAS collection, Hawker Siddeley Trident 2 E.

Clockwise from above The crew of Concorde 101, and the DAS welcoming committee, shortly after its arrival at Duxford airfield in August 1977. Among those gathered are the DAS chairman Don Selway, third from right, and famed Concorde test pilot Brian Trubshaw, sixth from right. © IWM MH 22898; The new and the old – Concorde overflies the de Havilland Dragon Rapide used for pleasure-flying by the Russavia Collection. © DAS; The first Concorde display at Duxford took place in 1982. © DAS

G-AVFB, on its retirement from British Airways, which performed a short display before landing. Almost 40,000 visitors had passed through the gates of the June show by early afternoon, and many other people watched from vantage points outside the airfield.

The special presence of Concorde at DAS-organised shows continued at the Duxford '84 display, with Concorde featuring not once, but twice. The charter flight organiser excelled himself and took enough

Concorde remains an icon today, and in the 1980s was the high point of any air show and many major public events.

bookings to fill the aircraft for two flights, so Concorde made two appearances during the afternoon. It displayed at the beginning of the show with its first load of passengers, before departing to carry out the supersonic part of the special charter flight over the sea. After landing at Heathrow to disembark those passengers and take on a new load, it then returned to Duxford to make its second appearance towards the end of the day.

The IWM Duxford '85 air show was jointly staged with the NSPCC, which was celebrating its centenary. Once again, DAS's Concorde charter arrangement was successful, and Concorde made an impressive appearance. One spectator was so moved by her first sighting of Concorde that she wrote to the local Cambridge newspaper describing her reaction. Under the headline 'Concorde made me want to cry', she wrote, 'I was dazzled, enchanted, awestruck. And when the unique and unmistakable silhouette of Concorde appeared over the western sky, it was as much as I could do not to cry. It is one of the most beautiful things I have ever seen – total grace, total power, total perfection.'

DAS is a Registered Charity and receives no official funding. It depends on the generosity of the public to preserve these iconic aircraft and welcomes new volunteers to help with their maintenance and presentation.

1990s

Duxford's Classic Years

DUXFORD'S GOLDEN MOMENTS: 1990s

The 1990 Duxford air show season began with the Classic Fighter Display, commemorating the 50th anniversary of the Battle of Britain, with dogfights of Spitfires, Hurricane and Buchóns much in evidence. Robs Lamplough's smoke generator-equipped Sea Fury made its UK flying debut, while the ever-larger 'Balbo' finale amassed some 25 warbirds in formation.

Further memorable moments at the dawn of the nineties came at Duxford '90, held on the Sunday of the Battle of Britain weekend in September. It attracted a record crowd at Duxford of nearly 39,500 on a single day. The finale was flown by the home-based father-and-son warbird teams, Ray and Mark Hanna of the Old Flying Machine Company and Stephen and Nick Grey of The Fighter Collection (TFC), consisting of two Spitfires and a Hurricane chasing a Buchón in its traditional Messerschmitt Bf 109 role. The Autumn Air Day saw *Sally B* flying in salute of the newly released Hollywood film *Memphis Belle*, in which it starred; joining it in formation were a Spitfire, Buchón, P-51 Mustang and Corsair.

For **1991**'s Classic Fighter Display, US Navy ace Lieutenant Alex Vraciu was present to watch TFC's Hellcat performing for the first time in his markings. Max Vogelsang's Swiss-based P-51D *Double Trouble Two* visited for its only UK appearance, flying as part of a show-opening Mustang four-ship. The long-awaited flying display debut of Messerschmitt Bf 109G-2 'Black 6', operated by IWM on behalf of the RAF, took place at Duxford '91 in September. During October's Autumn Air Day, the Bf 109 accompanied Spitfire LFXVIe RW382, restored for American collector David Tallichet by Historic Flying, on its first public flying appearance.

In **1992** the Classic Fighter Air Show expanded to two days and marked the 50th anniversary of the US Eighth and Ninth Air Forces arriving in Britain, attracting many American veterans. One of them was Maj Jack

Right A candid shot of an attendee reading the programme for the 1990 Classic Fighter Display air show. © IWM DUX 90/14/3

Top Four P-51D Mustangs opened the 1991 Classic Fighter Display, the familiar examples from the Old Flying Machine Company, Spencer Flack and Intrepid Aviation joined by Max Vogelsang's Swiss-based aircraft on its only ever UK outing. © Ben Dunnell; **Bottom** A sad end for the flying career of Bf 109 G-2 'Black 6', inverted in a field east of Duxford following the 1997 Autumn Air Show. Thankfully, the pilot escaped unhurt. © John Dunnell

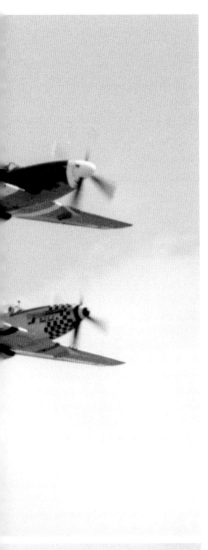

1993 was a momentous year of change and new beginnings at Duxford, with the first ever Flying Legends show opening the season on the May Day bank holiday.

Ilfrey, who saw TFC's recently arrived P-38J Lightning appearing in his markings. While Duxford '92 in September took place against a backdrop of low cloud and rain, those present were to see the last RAF Phantom to display at Duxford. By contrast, a beautiful October day saw TFC's Spitfire XIV enjoying its first display at the Autumn Air Show, while Lindsey Walton's Corsair and Plane Sailing's Tigercat flew their final performances prior to being exported to the USA.

1993 was a momentous year of change and new beginnings at Duxford, with the first ever Flying Legends show opening the season on the May Day bank holiday. Organised by TFC, the display was made up entirely of historic aircraft that were piston-powered and proved to be an immediate success. In turn, the final Classic Fighter Air Show took place in '93, being especially notable for the twin-engined formation of the Aircraft Restoration Company's freshly restored Blenheim, two B-25 Mitchells and BAe's Mosquito that brought up the rear of the traditional 'Balbo' flypast. A display by a US Air Force U-2R 'spyplane' was a very rare attraction at Duxford '93, before heavy rain set in for the rest of the programme.

The **1994** Duxford show calendar began with another major commemoration, the 50th anniversary of D-Day, and to mark this a combined air and military vehicle show was held on the first bank holiday in May. An inaugural two-day Flying Legends Air Show took place in July, and was a stunning occasion. The Fighter Collection brought together aircraft from many European operators previously unseen at any British event, the airfield attack scenario involving eight P-51 Mustangs and three B-25 Mitchells receiving particular praise. A new name for the September event saw Duxford '94 being dubbed the Family Air Show; in the air, the French Air Force team of two Mirage F1s – called Voltige Victor – put on a spectacular performance. Debuts for TFC's P-63A

Kingcobra and a genuine Fi 156 Storch, restored by Aero Vintage for the Italian Air Force Museum, at the Autumn Air Show brought a memorable end to the 1994 season.

1995 launched with a large crowd attending a show to celebrate the VE Day 50th anniversary on 8 May. It included a 1940s-style concert in one of the hangars, with a Winston Churchill look-alike in attendance and displays of military vehicles. In the air, several warbirds that were to take part in the VE Day anniversary flypast over Buckingham Palace launched from Duxford, while Hans Dittes' Bf 109G-10 arrived at the end of the show for operation by the Old Flying Machine Company (OFMC). In June, the OFMC staged its own display, the Midsummer Flying Day. Flying Legends cemented its place as Europe's best warbird event with yet more first appearances, like TFC's second Spitfire XIV, and Pino Valenti's Fiat G59 from Italy. Later in the year, a pair of US Air Force F-15Es, a Dassault Flamant and a BAe 146 freighter from TNT were among an eclectic mix at Duxford '95, while Spitfires were showcased at the Autumn Air Show.

By **1996** the Duxford season was packed with no fewer than five air shows in the year. On 6 May it launched with the Spitfire Diamond Jubilee Air Show to mark the 60th anniversary of the first flight by the prototype of the Supermarine fighter. More than 32,000 visitors watched what was claimed to be the largest ever post-Second World War gathering of Spitfires, with 21 examples of 10 different marks. Not all of them flew, but a nine-ship formation wowed the crowd in the air. The OFMC's show was enlarged into the Classic Jet and Fighter Display, at which vintage jets – such as Martin-Baker's ejection seat test Meteor, the Patrouille Cristaline Fouga Magister pair, a trio of Gnats and a quartet of Hunters – were given prominence like never before. The jets in the Heathrow Airport 50th anniversary flypast also diverted over Duxford that day – or, rather, most of them did, a few turning much too far to the south. Flying Legends was the biggest yet, with such spectacles as TFC's Spitfire V and newly delivered Tigercat making their debuts, a pair of Lysanders, four Skyraiders and no fewer than nine P-51s; the first day culminated in a record 39-warbird 'Balbo'. Regrettably, the weekend was marred on Sunday by the tragic loss of TFC's P-38, which killed pilot 'Hoof' Proudfoot.

The first show of **1997** moved to June, and was dubbed the Anniversary Air Show to celebrate 80 years since construction of RAF Duxford began. TFC's 'razorback' P-51C Mustang was the star of Flying Legends, while Duxford '97 was dominated by an American theme due to the 50th anniversary of the United States Air Force. The final display flight of Bf 109G-2 'Black 6' at the Autumn Air Show ended with a forced landing in a field east of the M11, and the aircraft on its back, but thankfully an unhurt pilot.

In **1998** the Spitfire Air Show boasted a record number of Spitfires and the biggest ever formation of the type flown at a modern UK air show, with 16 examples taking part in Sunday's mass finale in a close diamond formation. A never-repeated formation of three Lysanders was the highlight of the Flying Legends show. Duxford '98 went on to celebrate the 80th anniversary of the RAF, while the Autumn Air Show witnessed the Battle of Britain Memorial Flight's Hurricane LF363 returning to the air display circuit after a restoration.

The **1999** season, the last of the century, began with a May Air Display that focused on the Fleet Air Arm and the aircraft flown on D-Day. A very welcome visitor to Flying Legends was French-based B-17G *Pink Lady*, which had not displayed before at Duxford. September's Duxford '99 celebrated the progress and power of military aviation during the twentieth century. The Autumn Air Show was the last major UK air show of the millennium – it paid a highly poignant tribute to Old Flying Machine Company co-founder Mark Hanna, who had lost his life when the OFMC's Buchón crashed in Spain the previous month.

Right The late Reg Hallam flying the HA-1112 Buchón from the Charles Church fleet at 1990's Classic Fighter Display. © John Dunnell

LEGENDARY DAYS: FLYING LEGENDS AND DUXFORD

by Ben Dunnell

May Bank Holiday Monday in 1993 was when it all started. That inaugural one-day Flying Legends show was a fairly small affair, but the signs of something special were definitely there in The Fighter Collection (TFC)'s 'toe in the water' exercise. Today, looking back, its influence is not in doubt.

The same goes for its worldwide reputation. Air displays at IWM Duxford were nothing new by the time Flying Legends appeared on the calendar – indeed, they had been running for two decades – but it took TFC's historic aircraft extravaganza to put the venue on the international map. Aircraft operators and pilots, not to mention spectators, began beating a path to Duxford's door. The result, when Flying Legends became a two-day event

in its second year, was a spectacle that achieved new standards. It continued to do so.

With the growth of the UK warbird scene came the development of shows reflecting it. In the vanguard from 1982 was the Great Warbirds Air Display at West Malling, followed a couple of years later by the North Weald Fighter Meet. Both were genuinely pioneering. But even with its home-based

This page The largest Flying Legends 'Balbo' for some years was staged in 2018. © Harry Measures

"...this may not be to your liking but we're not going to bring in jets".

operators in the ascendancy, Duxford took a few years to follow. The Classic Fighter show, staged jointly by TFC and the Old Flying Machine Company in partnership with IWM, was the result. Held annually from 1989 it, too, set a high bar. The range of participating aircraft became ever wider, the flying increasingly spectacular. It was a heady combination.

Yet none of these displays – the first couple of Great Warbirds editions aside – were purely historic affairs. In understandably seeking broad appeal, they had introduced modern participation. All had present-day military involvement, while civil aerobatic acts, parachute teams and the occasional contemporary airliner were featured at Great Warbirds and the Fighter Meet. Was there room for something different?

Stephen Grey thought so. TFC's founder and boss had a concept in mind, one that sought to make more of Duxford's

potential as a venue. IWM's then Director of Duxford, Ted Inman, was keen for him to try it out. 'When I decided we were going to do it', Stephen recalled to the author in 2018, 'I said to Ted, "Look, this may not be to your liking but we're not going to bring in jets". It was a question of choreography. I'm not anti-jets – they're very exciting things – but Duxford is an historic airfield, we were only there because we had some historic aeroplanes and I believed the place was worthy of having an all-in historic aeroplane show, both military and civil.

'He asked whether I thought the public would come, because they like the noise and all the rest of it. I said, "Yes, that's exactly what I'm saying". If a jet comes roaring in and does an afterburning show and then we fly a Spitfire it is difficult to have somebody in awe of it. To a new visitor, it's just a small aircraft flying around, making little noise. If you have a Spitfire there all on its own, people will come to recognise a Spitfire and its wonderful sound. Ted agreed: "OK, fine,

have a go".'

That first one-day event in 1993 went ahead with only a little publicity. TFC had a new acquisition to showcase for the first time in the form of FM-2 Wildcat N4845V, the flying display's star attraction. A three-hour programme full of multi-aircraft sequences and mixed formations – and not just of warbirds, but classic civil types as well – ended with an RAF 75th anniversary warbird flypast, leaving the audience of more than 12,000 to go home very happy.

Flying Legends had defied any doubters. TFC also innovated considerably. The flightline walk was a Flying Legends creation, as later was the Gold Pass hospitality enclosure. The show's success demonstrated the potential of the early May Bank Holiday date, which IWM used successfully for several years. In time, parts of Flying Legends' non-stop style of flying display would be carried over into the other Duxford shows.

When the Classic Fighter show came to an end after its 1993 edition, it left a major gap in the Duxford calendar. The venue needed a warbird event. In Flying Legends there was already the ideal replacement. What's more, it had scope to develop. Holding it over two days – like Classic Fighter for its last two years – would help sharpen up everybody involved and make the whole affair more professional. Having researched potential dates, Stephen went for the second weekend in July. 'We needed a fresh crowd', he said. 'We also needed people who weren't just from around the Cambridge area.'

Much the same went for the aircraft. Stephen used the friendships and contacts he'd made around the European and US historic aircraft circuits to secure many machines never seen before on British shores. As he recalled, 'Some of them were afraid to come, some of them were delighted to come, some of them [continued] to come. At the time, to get the sort of aeroplanes we wanted to get together you couldn't have done it in England alone.'

With its inaugural two-day staging in 1994, Flying Legends came of age. Affording all due respect to what had gone hitherto, it established a new standard for historic aircraft displays. Nothing like it had ever been seen. The P-51D Mustangs set the tone – of the eight present, only those from TFC, Robs Lamplough and the Dutch Historic Aircraft Company had displayed in Britain before. The rest had not. Over from France were both of Flying Legend's examples, plus those from the Amicale Jean-Baptiste Salis and Air B Aviation. Completing the gathering after a late arrival from Sweden was Flygexpo's aircraft in Swedish Air Force markings. All were regulars at mainland European events, but to have them in one place was exceptional. The same went for Europe's three Mitchells, TFC's B-25D and the Dutch-based Duke of Brabant Air Force's B-25N joined by Flying Legend's B-25J. An Avenger on the Duxford flightline was nothing new, but for it to be Didier Chable's TBM-3E was. And the arrival of a P-40 in American Volunteer Group markings came as another surprise – it turned out to be the ex-TFC P-40M.

The line-up was exciting enough, the display itself even more so. No one who saw the eight-Mustang and three-Mitchell sequence that weekend is likely to forget it, the P-51s flying a dumbbell-pattern tailchase in one long stream while the B-25s rumbled past low and fast, bomb doors open. This, perhaps more than anything else, laid down the marker for things to come.

With different aircraft in different combinations, Flying Legends always presented something new. 'If you're trying to get a faithful audience, that's what you do', said Stephen. 'If you're the Drury Lane Theatre, you don't keep putting on *The Seagull*… but it gets more and more difficult to do.'

Everyone will have their own favourites. One that sticks firmly in the mind is 1998's trio of Lysanders, provided by the Aircraft Restoration Company, Shuttleworth and the Sabena Old Timers. Part of the show's Bristol Mercury-powered combine alongside Blenheim and Gladiator, long a staple item, this was a true one-off – first the ARC-operated example was sold to Kermit Weeks,

Clockwise from top Flying Legends show founder Stephen Grey gave his last flying displays at a British event in 2013, choosing the Bearcat as his mount. © Ben Dunnell; Christophe Jacquard's Flug Werk FW 190 only visited once, for the 2009 show, but was a memorable star item. It carried out low-level passes with the Buchón owned by Tom Blair. © Ben Dunnell; For many years, this spectacle would have been scarcely believable, but it happened in 2011: four Hawker biplanes in close company. Leading was Howell Davis's Demon; flanking it were the Nimrods of The Fighter Collection and the Historic Aircraft Collection, with Shuttleworth's Hind bringing up the rear. © Ben Dunnell

'It was noisy, unpredictable but always... bloody exciting.'

then, a few years later, Sabena's was damaged in a mishap. Flown by Lee Proudfoot, 'Dodge' Bailey and Jean-Michel Legrand, the three 'Lizzies' made a scarcely believable sight, especially as they split in a head-on 'bomb-burst'.

There have been many others, of course. Memorable multiples of Grummans, Rapides, Bristol Fighters, Hawker biplanes, Buchóns and more have contributed much to Legends' lustre. But so have some of its regular elements. One of the most memorable used to be the 'Ultimate Pistons' tailchase, Ray Hanna in the OFMC's Iraqi Fury, Stephen Grey in TFC's Bearcat. For a while there were two Bearcats, the collection's second example joining in the joust with Paul Bonhomme at the helm. It once gave cause for commentator Jerry Mead to exclaim, 'This is just *wonderful*.'

Stephen recalled, 'Ray would brief saying it was an air show act, it's not two boys having a "go", but he always turned it

into a "knife fight", always. I don't know why – maybe it was just because Ray was a great professional, trying to stretch me as a part-timer out of my personal envelope. It was noisy, unpredictable but always "in his six", safe but bloody exciting – I think that's why people remember it.'

No air show is without its trials and tribulations. Often they remain hidden from the public's view; sometimes, though, they cannot help but become apparent. That was the case in 2009, when a bureaucratic issue during the months running up to Legends grounded all TFC's British-registered aircraft. It was a major blow, but that year's show turned out to be one of the best, adversity or no. And if ever an opening gambit caught the attention, 2009's was it. Making what turned out to be its only appearance, Christophe Jacquard's Flug Werk FW 190A-8/N beat up the airfield in the finest style, the late Marc 'Léon' Mathis at the controls of the reproduction Focke-Wulf Fw 190. With it, Brian Smith in Tom

Below Always one of the best displays on the scene: Ray Hanna in the Fury, Stephen Grey in the Bearcat. © Andrew Read

Blair's Hispano Buchón made a Luftwaffe fighter duo as seven Spitfires wheeled about behind. Were one to pick a sequence that best encapsulates the show, this might be it.

There were other motivations behind the event, though. 'The principal reason I was doing it', said Stephen Grey, 'was that some elderly Second World War pilots that I knew were beginning to become unhealthy and possibly were going to die quite soon. The idea was to try and honour them without dragging them round like they're "pigs in a fête". We spent a lot of time lifting public awareness of the living heroes… in the process we made friends of many really courageous, wonderful but humble pilots. Most of them are gone now. Those are the memories I most treasure'. Many distinguished attendees resulted, among them such great names as Alex Henshaw, 'Johnnie' Johnson, 'Bud' Anderson, 'Winkle' Brown and others.

Another was Roland Beamont, a man with close Duxford connections through his wartime service with No. 609 Squadron on the Typhoon. He had become TFC's honorary safety pilot, imparting a great deal of first-hand advice. Following his death in 2001, the Belgian government decided to make the posthumous award to 'Bee' of the country's Croix de Guerre, honouring his time in command of 609 when it had many Belgian pilots on strength. The venue for the presentation to Beamont's daughters was Flying Legends 2003, with a significant number of 609 veterans in attendance. The presence of such men was as valued as that of any aeroplane, if not more.

In 2013, Stephen decided to make Flying Legends the scene of his last UK displays. One slot, above all, had become his own: the 'Joker', filling the gaps while the 'Balbo' finale formed up, and between its first and second passes. For this his main mount was the Bearcat, with powerful performances of penetrating aerobatics. Choosing the Grumman fighter as his valedictory steed, this time Stephen opened the show, his immaculate demonstrations set to Pink Floyd's *Shine On You Crazy Diamond*. Later each day, the baton was passed to his son Nick, who took the 'Joker' role in TFC's Gladiator II. Against a peerless evening sky, Nick put on a simply spellbinding display, the silver biplane being flown in a manner probably not witnessed since its service heyday. More magic moments.

Following the cancellation of 2020's show due to the COVID-19 pandemic, there came an announcement stating that Flying Legends would no longer be held at Duxford, and that TFC was to seek an alternative venue. In 2023 this was announced as Leeds East Airport, the former RAF Church Fenton. But as a new era for Flying Legends opens, so recollections of its unrivalled place in Duxford's air show history will always remain.

This feature is adapted from an article by Ben Dunnell in the May 2018 issue of *Aeroplane* magazine.

'In the 1990s, three Corsairs – a favourite of mine – were flying. My partner and I secured a fantastic spot perched on the crash-gate spot to watch. At the end of the display, Lindsey Walton, the pilot of one of the Corsairs, walked over towards our section of the crash-gate. We caught his eye and engaged him in conversation about his aircraft. Taken by our enthusiasm, he uncoupled the section of crash-gate we were nestled up against and said, "come with me". He showed us around the aircraft from the ground, and then to my never-ending disbelief, he asked if I would like to look inside her cockpit. I was on the wing in a flash and leaned over to peer inside. As the aircraft had only just landed, the cockpit was still hot, and it smelled of hot leather and engine oil. It was absolutely wonderful.'

Elizabeth Hodder

'I remember the Classic Jet and Fighter Display air show involving the spectacular civil airliner flypast making its way to Heathrow in 1996. The pure adrenalin of seeing a Boeing 747 and Concorde, to name but a few, has to be a highlight.'

Richard Billington-Howes

Clockwise from top The first of the two PBY-5A Catalinas operated from Duxford by Plane Sailing flies past at Flying Legends 1994 with Didier Chable's TBM-3E Avenger, one of many overseas-based warbirds which made their debuts at that show. © Ben Dunnell; The Fighter Collection's founding aircraft, the P-51D named *Candyman/Moose*, takes off during the 1992 Classic Fighter Air Show. © John Dunnell; Spitfires almost as far as the eye can see in May 1998, headed by a replica of the first prototype. © Ben Dunnell; The late Lindsey Walton, who died in 2019, at the controls of his F4U-7 Corsair in French Navy markings. © PRM Aviation Collection

Mark Hanna of The Old Flying Machine Company relates his experiences flying the OFMC Messerschmitt 109J.

Track around the canopy through Nine, Eleven and now Twelve O'Clock. Rolling out gently now the specks are becoming objects and I can see wings and start to discern fuselages and engines. We're at five miles and closing at 420 knots and greater than seven miles a minute. Less then 50 seconds to go. There's the '51 escort high and behind the bombers. Good... they're not a factor for the inital attack, but we will need to worry about them on the egress. 20 seconds and two miles. I've picked my target – the lead ship... I've misjudged the attack slightly, just missed the dead 180 so I've got a slight crosser which is going to foul up my sighting situation. 10 seconds to run... the B-17s light up! Flashes from all over the airframes and smoke trails streak behind as the gunners let rip and fill the skies with lead. They're out of range but it's still frightening. The lead ship is filling my windscreen and closing rapidly. Now... Fire! Two second burst... flash. flash. flash... HITS!... all in his cockpit and fuselage area... pull slightly on the control column to just clear his port wing, the fin slicing past just by me and roll hard left. World, B-17s gyrating round, stop inverted... pull 5Gs, nose down, down, down, streamers pouring from the wingtips. I've lost the P-51's. I can't see them but I know they'll be after us. I'm out of here vertically down with a windscreen full of ground, rolling as I go to spoil any pursuing Mustangs' sighting solutions – straight towards the Fatherland... only it isn't – it's Suffolk and Ron's calling... "Jimmy says can we do that one again Mark...".

This is David Puttnam's Memphis Belle and we are airborne with five B-17's, seven P-51's, three '109's and a B-25. I'm leading the '109 formation. We're short on gas, it's cold at 12,000 feet and this is fantastic, tremendous fun. The Me109 is, without doubt, the most satisfying and challenging aircraft that I have ever flown. So how does it fly and how does it compare with other World War II fighters?

Mark Hanna piloting the OFMC's Me 109J over Cambridgeshire J Rigby

FLYING THE '109

To my eye, the aircraft looks dangerous; both to the enemy and to its own pilots. The aircraft's difficult reputation is well known and right from the outset you are aware that it is an aeroplane that needs to be treated with a great deal of respect. Talk to people about the '109 and all you hear about is how you are going to wrap it up on take-off or landing! As you walk up to the '109 one is at first struck by the small size of the aircraft, particularly if parked next to a contemporary American fighter. Closer examination reveals a crazy looking knock-kneed undercarriage, a very heavily framed sideways opening canopy with almost no forward view in the three point attitude, a long rear fuselage and tiny tail surfaces. A walk-round reveals ingenious split radiator flaps which double as an extension to the landing flaps, ailerons with a lot of movement and rather odd looking external mass balances. Also independently operating leading edge slats, these devices should glide open and shut on the ground with the pressure of a single finger. Other unusual features include the horizontal stabilizer doubling as the elevator trimmer and the complete absence of a rudder trim system. Overall the finish is a strange mix of innovative and archaic.

Climbing on board you have to be careful not to stand on the radiator flap, then lower yourself gently downwards and forwards, taking your weight by holding onto the windscreen. Once in you are aware that you are almost lying down in the aeroplane, the position reminicent of a racing car. The cockpit is very narrow and if you have broad shoulders (don't all fighter pilots?) it is a tight squeeze. Once strapped in, itself a knuckle wrapping affair, you can take stock. First impressions are of simplicity and straight forwardness. Next close the canopy to check the seating position. Normally, if you haven't flown to '109 before you get a clout on the head as you swing the heavy lid over and down. Nobody sits that low in a fighter! To start, power ON, boost pumps ON. Three good shots on the very stiff primer. Set the throttle about ½ inch open. "CLEAR PROP". It's a good start and with a brief snort of flame the '109 fires up immediately. One is immediately aware that the aeroplane is "Rattley"; engine, canopy, reduction gear all provide little vibrations and shakes transmitted directly to the pilot.

Power up to 1800 RPM and suddenly we're rolling... to turn, stick forward against the instrument panel to lighten the tail. A blast of throttle and a jab of brake. Do this in a Spitfire and you are on your nose! Forward view can only be described as appalling, and due to the tail/brake arrangement this makes weaving more

FLYING THE '109

difficult than on other similar types. Oil temperature is 30°, coolant temperature is greater than or at 60°. Brakes hard on (there is no parking brake), stick back and power gently up. The noise and vibration levels have now increased dramatically. Power back down to 1800 RPM and check the mags. We must hurry as the coolant temperature is at 98°C and going UP – we have to get rolling to get some cooling air through the radiators. Pre-take off checks... Elevator trim set to +1°, no rudder trim, throttle friction light. This is vital as I'm going to need to use my left hand for various services immediately after take-off. Mixture is automatic, pitch fully fine... Fuel/Oil cock is ON, both boost pumps are ON, pressure is good, primer is done up. Flaps – crank down to 20° for take off. Rad flaps checked at full open; if we take off with them closed we will certainly boil the engine and guaranteed to crack a head. Gyro's set to Duxford's runway. Instruments; temps and pressures all in the green for take off. Radiator is now 102°. Oxygen we don't have, hood re-checked down and locked, harness tight and secure, hydraulics select down in the gear and pressurise the system check 750 psi. Controls full and free, tail wheel locked. Got to go – 105°. There's no time to hang around and worry about the take off. Here we go... Power gently up and keep it coming smoothly... it's VERY noisy! Keep the tail down initially, keep it straight by feel rather than any positive technique... tail coming up now... once the rudders effective. Unconscious corrections to the rudder are happening all the time. It's incredibly entertaining to watch the '109 take off or land. The rudder literally flashes around!

The little fighter is now bucketing along, accelerating rapidly. Now the tail's up and you can see vaguely where you are going. It's a rough, wild, buckety ride on grass and with noise, smoke from the stacks and the aeroplane bouncing around it's exciting! Quick glance at the ASI – 100 mph, slight check back on the stick and we're flying.

Hand off the throttle, rotate the gear selector and activate the hydraulic button. The mechanical indicators motor up very quickly and you feel a clonk, clonk as the gear comes home. 130 mph and an immediate climbing turn up and right onto the downwind leg just in case I need to put the aeroplane down in a hurry. Start to frantically crank the flap up – now up the speeds. Plenty of airflow through the narrow radiators now, so close them and remember to keep a careful eye on the coolant gauge for the next few minutes until the temperature has settled down. With the rad flaps closed the aircraft accelerates positively. Level off and power back. The speed's picked up to the '109s cruise of about 235-240 mph and now the tail is right in the middle and no rudder input is necessary.

J Rigby

Once settled down with adrenalin level back down to just high, we can take stock of our situation. The initial reaction is of delight to be flying a classic aeroplane, and next the realisation that this is a real fighter. You feel aggressive flying it. The urge is to go looking for something to bounce and shoot down.

The roll rate is very good and very positive below about 250 mph. Above 250 mph however the roll starts to heavy up and up to 300 or so is very similar to a P-51. After that it's all getting pretty solid and you need two hands on the stick for any meaningful roll rates.

Pitch is also delightful at 250 mph and below. It feels very positive and the amount of effort on the control column needed to produce the relevant nose movement seems exactly right to me. The aircraft delights in being pulled into hard manuoeuvering turns at these slower speeds.

Initial acceleration is rapid, particularly with nose down, up to about 320 mph. After that the '109 starts to become a little reluctant and you have to be fairly determined to get over 350-360 mph. So how does the aeroplane compare with other contemporary fighters? First, let me say that all my comments are based on operations below 10,000 feet and at power settings not exceeding +12 (54″) and 2700 rpm. I liked it as an aeroplane and with familiarity I think it will give most of the allied fighters I have flown a hard time, particularly in a close, hard turning, slow speed dog-fight. It will definitely out-manoeuvre a P-51 in this type of fight, the roll rate and slow speed characteristics being much better. The Spitfire on the other hand is more of a problem for the '109 and I feel it is a superior close in

fighter. Having said that the aircraft are sufficiently closely matched that pilot ability would probably be the deciding factor. At higher speeds the P-51 is definitely superior, and provided the Mustang kept his energy up and refused to dogfight he would be relatively safe against the '109. There's no doubt that when you are flying the '109 and you look out and see the crosses on the wings you feel aggressive; if you are in an allied fighter it is very intimidating to see this dangerous little aeroplane turning in on you!

Mark Hanna

This is an extract from the article 'Flying the '109' wich appeared in issue number eleven of Warbirds Worldwide.

If anyone as any Me109 parts for sale or trade please contact Mark Hanna at the Old Flying Machine Company. Telephone 44 (0) 728 723622.

THE HANNAS: AVIATORS SUPREME

by Ben Dunnell

I n the development of Duxford's air shows and the airfield's warbird scene, the late Ray and Mark Hanna were outstanding figures. And to generations of aficionados, the mere mention of Supermarine Spitfire IX MH434 conjures memories of outstanding flying and legendary names.

This page Mark (left) and Ray Hanna, founders of the OFMC. © Jim Empson

That derives in part from its wartime combat history – 79 operational sorties in total, and two-and-a-half aerial kills in the hands of Flight Lieutenant Henry Lardner-Burke DFC with No. 222 Squadron. But it also stems from its association with the unforgettable father-and-son duo of Ray and Mark Hanna, two of the pilots who gave Duxford its particular aura, and key figures both in its expansion as a centre of warbird operation. Thanks to them, the venue witnessed some of its finest flying moments.

Already renowned for his then unprecedented four seasons as leader of the RAF Aerobatic Team, the Red Arrows, Ray Hanna was first acquainted with MH434 in February 1970. The New Zealander had been invited to fly the Spitfire by its then owner, Cathay Pacific director Sir Adrian Swire, and soon he was displaying it in the superlative style he made his own. That was never to change.

During 1981, Ray and his son Mark – then still a serving RAF officer, who flew the Phantom air defence fighter on frontline duty – co-founded the Old Flying Machine Company (OFMC), along at that stage with air-to-air photographer Arthur Gibson and RAF pilot John Watts. Based at Duxford, initially it operated a Max-Holste Broussard and Pilatus P2. The acquisition that would be key to the OFMC's future, however, came in 1983. Spitfire MH434 was put up for sale in a Christie's auction, Duxford coincidentally its location, and Ray Hanna was determined to acquire it on behalf of a consortium. Despite a late counterbid, they were successful. MH434 was integrated into the OFMC, and the invitation to base the aeroplane at Duxford was accepted with alacrity. As still more aircraft joined the fleet, covering everything from First World War types to classic jets, so they too bolstered the ranks of airworthy warbirds that called the airfield home.

So active was the company with display and film work through the 1980s and '90s that, at

the height of a typical season, it was rare to find all its charges there at once. But there was still an important contribution to be made to Duxford's own events, whether through aircraft appearances or organisationally. It was the OFMC that, in 1986, put together the inaugural Classic Fighter Display. When it was next staged during 1989, Classic Fighter was run in co-operation with The Fighter Collection, and a terrific series of shows followed. This, very much, was the historic-focused spectacular with widespread visiting participation that Duxford merited.

The final Classic Fighter show took place in July 1993. But this was far from the end of OFMC events at Duxford. To mark MH434's 50th anniversary, it staged a special celebration later that same month, with Spitfire test pilot Alex Henshaw among the guests of honour to watch a small flying display. A 1994 flying day raised money for the Lord's Taverners. For 1995, things were taken a step further, the Midsummer Flying Day adopting a June slot in the calendar and expanding into a full-scale air show. Even better was to follow in 1996, the OFMC's Classic Jet and Fighter Display bringing together Duxford's largest line-up of vintage jets. Performances from such as Martin-Baker's ejection seat test Meteor, and a trio of Gnats, were exceptional; the quartet of Hunters, led by two ex-Swiss examples newly arrived with OFMC, capped off a memorable day.

Those who flew for, and alongside, the Hannas look back on the experience with special fondness. Paul Bonhomme, later to become a multiple Red Bull Air Race world champion, began his association with OFMC during the 1990s. He says, 'I'll never forget one display at Duxford where they said I was flying a Mustang, and I was going to be paired up with Ray Hanna. I'd obviously met Ray, but I'd never flown with him. I thought, "Bloody hell, now I really do have to start behaving". I met up with Ray on the tower; we stood on the little balcony, and he said, "Hey, Paul, what do you want to do – lead or follow?" Not a question you get asked every day. I said, "Why don't you do exactly what you want to do and I'll follow, or if you want me to lead I'll lead? You choose". He said, "Alright, I'll lead, you sit in echelon starboard somewhere, don't go below me and don't go above me". That was

basically the brief.

'B-17 Sally B was going to be flying at the same time, and the "don't go below me and don't go above me" bit became apparent when we came hurtling round the corner, turning down 06. I was following Ray, and I thought I'd have a little look out for situational awareness. As we rolled wings level, coming the other way was Sally B. We went between the B-17 and the ground, and it wasn't a very big gap. It was fantastic. I followed Ray in various displays, and he was just super, super-smooth. There wasn't a corner in sight.'

Rolf Meum, too, enjoyed many exceptional times at Duxford flying the OFMC's aircraft. 'If we'd had a long working day or two and it was beautiful weather, the Spitfire, the Mustang or something would be sitting out on the ramp, and at the end of the day we'd decide to go and have a flight. We'd go five minutes out the back, dogfight like crazy and come in to land. After one of these, with Ray, Mark and myself, we couldn't help ourselves from doing a few flypasts when we came back to Duxford. We landed – it was a bit after-hours – and we saw [airfield manager] David Henchie coming round the corner. Ray was standing there and, seeing the way Henchie was walking towards us, said, "I think we're in the shit". We seemed to be in the shit a lot! But we had some fantastic times. Those were golden years at Duxford.

'One summer I did 75 hours on Spitfires. We had such high currency at the OFMC. There was one day when I flew five different types: I started by air-testing the Fury, then a flight in the Harvard, a display in the MiG, then the Mustang and finishing up in the Hunter.'

Already a seasoned warbird pilot back home in New Zealand, Keith Skilling started displaying for the Duxford-based operators during the English summers. For him, being teamed up with Ray Hanna was an education. 'Ray taught me a hell of a lot about display flying', he says, 'not by sitting down and talking but just by following and watching him leading. It was a different way of doing things.'

That became abundantly clear to all who had the pleasure of joining him in the Breitling Fighters team, the aerobatic four-ship of warbirds backed by Swiss watch company Breitling that debuted in 1999.

Cliff Spink generally flew the FG-1D Corsair in the slot position, directly behind Ray in the P-40E Kittyhawk. The sheer artistry of the former Red Arrows leader was something to marvel at. 'Ray was a consummate leader', Cliff says. 'He was so intuitive, he was so in touch with the other aeroplanes in his formation'. One of Ray's typically laconic radio calls from the Breitling days remains in Cliff's mind: 'We were doing a practice, he was tightening on something, and he said, "Don't chew my tail off, Air Marshal."'

The end of the Breitling Fighters' inaugural season brought the most desperate tragedy, when Mark Hanna lost his life in an accident to the OFMC's Buchón at Sabadell, Spain. One of the company's guiding lights, one of the most inspired pilots ever to be seen displaying historic aeroplanes, was gone. Stoical as ever in the face of such sadness, his father Ray carried on. He led the Breitling team until that contract ended with a final appearance at New Zealand's Warbirds over Wanaka show at Easter 2004, and displayed MH434 with undimmed panache up to the end of the 2005 season. Then Ray died, at home in Switzerland, on 1 December 2005. He was 77.

It had been a glorious October day when, at Duxford's Autumn Air Show in 1999, tribute was paid to Mark. The OFMC closed the afternoon's programme, beginning with a 'missing man' formation of the L-39 Albatros and the Breitling Fighters, ending with the piston warbird four-ship, Ray at its helm. What turned out to be Ray's last flight took place in equally peerless late-season skies, at 2005's Autumn Air Show. There in MH434 he led Cliff Spink through a two-ship aerobatic Spitfire sequence of the highest class. Fast-forward to September 2019, and the Battle of Britain Air Show. To honour 20 years since Mark's passing, MH434 was flown through a simply spellbinding routine by Brian Smith, a man whose association with the Hannas, the OFMC and its most illustrious aeroplane means a great deal.

Today, the company is run by Sarah Hanna – daughter of Ray, sister of Mark. And MH434 is flown absolutely in their spirit. Countless Spitfires have graced Duxford over its air show seasons. None quite have the lustre of this one.

Above The Old Flying Machine Company's famous Spitfire IX MH434, being flown by Lee Proudfoot. © Ben Dunnell; **Below** Ray Hanna's last display: the maestro leads Cliff Spink in a two-ship Spitfire aerobatic sequence. © Ben Dunnell

BATTLE
ANNIVE
5

FREE
COMPETITION
See centre
pages

PR·D

XFORD
Imperial War Museum

IMPERIAL WAR
MUSEUM

81

2000s

Duxford's New Millennium

591

DUXFORD'S GOLDEN MOMENTS: 2000s

 The 2000s launched with a Flying Legends show laden with debuts. The Fighter Collection's repainted Spitfire FRXIVe saluted AVM 'Johnnie' Johnson, the show's guest of honour, and was flown spectacularly by Paul Bonhomme.

JCB Aviation's P-51D Mustang *Nooky Booky IV*, Air B Aviation's Bearcat and Christophe Jacquard's Yak-9 were all visiting from France for the first time; likewise Historic Invader Aviation's A-26C *Hard To Get* came over from the Netherlands, while TFC's and Shuttleworth's Bristol Fighters flew together at last. The Battle of Britain Anniversary Air Show, held that September, saw a record-breaking gathering of 22 Spitfires, with 19 flying at the same time. The BBMF 'Spits' gave a separate formation display while the rest, plus three Hurricanes, formed up in a loose 'Big Wing'-style gaggle for a crowd-rear arrival. The Autumn Air Show marked the 50th anniversary of the start of the Korean War. It was the last chance to see Meteor F8 VZ467 before its sale by Kennet Aviation to a new Australian owner.

Kicking off the Duxford season with a splendid start, the May Air Display of **2001** saw de Havilland Aviation's Sea Vixen XP924 give its first display as part of a wider de Havilland theme, a cavalcade of other types welcoming the establishment at the airfield of de Havilland Support. At Flying Legends, Grumman F3F and G-32A biplanes from the Friedkin family collection were brought over from California for a unique appearance, flying in a mass formation of designs by the famous American manufacturer. Come September, army aviation was the theme of the perishingly cold Duxford 2001 show. Highlights included brilliant solo and pairs routines from the Army Air Corps' new Apache attack helicopters. The Autumn Air Show paid a fitting tribute to women in aviation as Jeanne Frazer took over as

Right The South African Airways Boeing 747-400 over Duxford at the Centenary of Flight air show in 2003. © Peter R March

...the Centenary of Flight Air Show celebrated aviation's greatest anniversary milestone with Duxford's most varied line-up ever.

Duxford's first female Flying Display Director.

The **2002** season was full of spectacular anniversaries. The opening Jubilee Air Show celebrated the Queen's Golden Jubilee with a regal display of aircraft with Royal connections. The year also saluted the 20th anniversary of the Falklands War with a formation of Westland Wasp and Scout, Boeing Chinook and Westland Puma helicopters. Flying Legends displayed an A-36A Apache from the Friedkin collection; it was specially shipped over for the show and became the first Allison-engined Mustang variant to fly in Britain since wartime. Duxford 2002 marked the 60th anniversary of the Eighth Air Force arriving in Britain with a natural focus on *Sally B*.

Strong winds affected the May Air Display in **2003** but it paid tribute to 'Against the Odds' missions of the Second World War, with a nod to the 60th anniversary of the famous Dambusters raid. The loss of the RN Historic Flight's Firefly, along with its two crew, marred this year's Flying Legends. The rest of the show included the debut display by the OFMC's Lavochkin La-9, and a unique formation of TFC's P-47M and newly restored P-51D *Twilight Tear*, Rob Davies' P-51D *Big Beautiful Doll*, and the Friedkins' Cavalier TF-51D, all in 78th Fighter Group markings. In September, the Centenary of Flight Air Show celebrated aviation's greatest anniversary milestone with Duxford's most varied line-up ever. The amazingly agile South African Airways Boeing 747-400 display grabbed the attention of all, and was complemented by a one-off 'Duxford 100' formation of 13 warbirds spelling out '100' in

the air. Christian Moullec led a bizarre but memorable formation in his microlight with a dozen geese. He had skilfully trained the geese to regard the microlight as their 'mother' and follow the aircraft around the sky. A rather more familiar formation, the OFMC's Breitling Fighters warbird team, bowed out from the British circuit at the Autumn Air Show.

In **2004** a huge crowd turned out for the D-Day Anniversary Air Show and were dazzled by a range of period-appropriate warbirds. After a long restoration, TFC's P-39Q Airacobra debuted at Flying Legends; following an even longer (27-year) restoration, David and Mark Miller's superb Dragon Rapide appeared for the first time, leading six-ship Rapide 70th anniversary flypasts. The star overseas attendee was the Polikarpov I-15bis from Aviarestoration in Russia. The Rolls-Royce centenary and the 70th anniversary of the sinking of the *Tirpitz* themed the Duxford Air Show, with the latter marked by the BBMF Lancaster and No. 617 Squadron Tornados in loose formation. The Autumn Air Show had became a truly major event by this point, with large-scale RAF and Royal Navy participation an annual standard.

In **2005** the two-day VE Day Anniversary Air Show was poignantly held over the actual anniversary weekend. Despite bad weather, the show still featured the post-restoration debuts of Peter Vacher's Hurricane I and Historic Flying's Spitfire IXT. Flying Legends was bigger than ever before, the official VE Day anniversary flypast over Buckingham Palace being launched out of the show on Sunday afternoon. The Swedish Air Force Museum sent its Saab B 17 dive-bomber for

Left No other Duxford display item has been anything like Christian Moullec's combination of a microlight and geese, as seen at the 2003 Centenary of Flight show. © Jeanne Frazer

its first, and so far only, British displays, while Stephen Grey was at the controls of TFC's Hawk 75 for its spectacular post-restoration debut. The Battle of Britain 65th Anniversary Air Show in September gathered many Spitfires and Hurricanes, but the flying was restricted on Saturday by bad weather and called off altogether on Sunday. During the Spitfire finale of the Autumn Air Show, the great Ray Hanna gave what turned out to be his last public display before his death in December – fittingly, at the controls of his beloved MH434.

The **2006** AirSpace Air Show featured an array of aircraft types to be exhibited in IWM Duxford's newly constructed AirSpace building. Three Bristol Fighters, including the first air show appearance of the Historic Aircraft Collection's newly restored example, offered a truly historic sight at Flying Legends. Later in the year, the Spitfire 70th Anniversary Air Show marked the type's maiden flight in 1936. The Autumn Air Show hosted a superb international line-up, including the French Air Force Patrouille de France team's first Duxford appearance since 1975, now flying Alpha Jets; the Belgian Air Component provided its last UK display of a Fouga Magister, and an F-16 Fighting Falcon which flew in formation with Historic Flying's Spitfire XVIII.

2007 was another year of firsts at Duxford. A special event in early May, the BBMF Day, paid tribute to the 50th anniversary of the RAF's Battle of Britain Memorial Flight – all its airworthy machines attended, and the flying was closed by a formation of Lancaster, two Hurricanes and five Spitfires. The first jet appearance at a Flying Legends show was made by the USAF F-15E Strike Eagle Demo Team, and the exciting launch of the American Air Day brought USAF displays in the air and on the ground, with numerous Mildenhall and Lakenheath-based assets attending, such as the very rare sight of an HH-60G Pave Hawk combat rescue helicopter.

B-17G *Liberty Belle* crossed the Atlantic to attend the **2008** Flying Legends as part of a short UK tour, and formed a three-aircraft Flying Fortress line-up alongside *Pink Lady* and *Sally B*. Wet and windy weather once again came into play at the Duxford Anniversary Air Show, which marked the 90th anniversary of both the airfield and the RAF. Nevertheless, the crowds were treated to an excellent Spitfire 'diamond nine' display, the return of Vulcan XH558 to the venue – now in civilian hands – and a trio of C-47s.

For **2009**, the Spring Air Show was themed around 'Best of British', with famous aircraft and pilots on the bill. Despite a paperwork issue meaning most of TFC's own fleet was unable to take part, Flying Legends proved an absolute triumph, Christophe Jacquard's Flug Werk FW 190A/8-N – a 'new-build' Focke-Wulf Fw 190 – being the high point of extensive foreign warbird participation. The Duxford Air Show celebrated Britain's hosting (at Silverstone) of the World Aerobatic Championships, with four top pilots flying a 'demonstration competition' in vintage machines. The Air Transport Auxiliary was saluted at the Autumn Air Show with a first-time combined display of a Hurricane and Spitfire flown by female pilots, namely Anna Walker and Carolyn Grace.

Above A gathering of heroes at Flying Legends in 2001: from left to right, Second World War aces 'Bud' Anderson, Pete Brothers, Lee Archer, Bob Goebel and Don Blakeslee. © Ben Dunnell; **Below** Visiting from across the Atlantic, the Liberty Foundation's B-17G *Liberty Belle* is sandwiched between two other Flying Fortresses: *Sally B*, which was not flying at the time due to an engine problem, and the French-owned *Pink Lady*. © Ben Dunnell

AAAH...
DE HAVILLAND!

by Ben Dunnell

Members of the recently formed Duxford Aviation Society were understandably excited in August 1975. Next summer, they hoped, they'd have on a long lease an airworthy de Havilland Dragon Rapide to ride in and display. The twin-engined biplane airliner, registered G-AGJG, was duly ferried up from Biggin Hill.

But soon it became apparent that the dilapidated machine, most recently used as a parachute jump platform and stored outdoors, required far deeper restoration than had yet been attempted with this type. When the Rapide did take to the skies again, on 19 June 2004, it was 27 years after its rebuild began in earnest, and by now owned by David and Mark Miller, father and son, who had been instrumental in getting the project under way. It ranks among Duxford's finest ever restorations, and has fittingly been a feature of many IWM air shows. But its significance is broader than that.

One begins to get an idea of why from the fact that Mark Miller is today chief engineer of de Havilland Support Ltd, the organisation which provides continuing airworthiness services for many of the famous manufacturer's piston-engined types, and is based on the north side of the A505 road that divides the IWM Duxford site. He's been around the airfield since before its earliest museum days, initially engaging in aeromodelling activities alongside his parents. Mark and David set to work on G-AGJG during 1977, with, says Mark, 'no real on-aircraft experience at all... Translating my interest to a practical level came purely through the Rapide'. Engineering degrees and CAA Aircraft Maintenance Engineer's Licences came much later, greatly influenced by the project.

Along the way, he learned to fly on tailwheel-equipped historic aeroplanes, going solo on a Tiger Moth with the Cambridge Flying Group in 1981, and

Above Mark Miller at the controls of G-AGJG during a local sortie from Duxford. © Harry Measures. **Below** DH89A Dragon Rapide G-AGJG, which took 27 years to restore, being displayed by Mark Miller. © Ben Dunnell

completing his private pilot's licence in the Duxford-based Auster Autocrat G-AGTO. The Millers purchased the Rapide outright during 1986, thus securing its future. Mark's story of how he badgered the previous owner into selling is a colourful tale in itself. Progress in workshop space provided by IWM was gradual but meticulous, the result an outstanding example of the breed. G-AGJG was finished in colours unique for any airworthy aircraft in the world: its original wartime markings as worn with the Northern Division of Scottish Airways, combining RAF camouflage with civil registration.

Just weeks after its maiden post-restoration flight, by Henry Labouchere, came Flying Legends 2004. Not only was the Rapide scheduled to give its debut display there, but it did so at the head of a six-ship formation of the type, which celebrated its 70th anniversary that year. Lee Proudfoot was at the controls of G-AGJG; behind it, two others came from the Duxford-based Classic Wings pleasure-flying fleet, a further pair from Air Atlantique, and the sixth courtesy of Ken Whitehead. Watching it all happen, Mark wrote, 'My mind wandered involuntarily to all the sunny days spent cooped up in the workshop, to foggy drives home after late-night winter sessions, and I shook my head in disbelief at what was now unfolding.'

Such a marvellous spectacle has never been repeated. Many others have, however. Both David and Mark converted to type a few weeks afterwards, and in early 2005 Mark upgraded his display authorisation – gained after

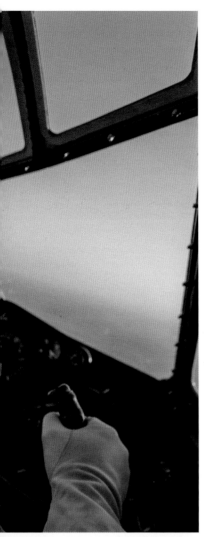

Duxford... 'the one venue in the wide world where all this could have happened'.

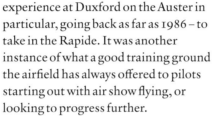

experience at Duxford on the Auster in particular, going back as far as 1986 – to take in the Rapide. It was another instance of what a good training ground the airfield has always offered to pilots starting out with air show flying, or looking to progress further.

His first public appearance at the controls was at the 2005 VE Day Anniversary Air Show, on its second day performing in concert with a Beech 18. Over the years, Mark and the Rapide have been enlisted to lead an assortment of the mixed formations that are such a distinctive feature of Duxford, often one-offs. 'It's a very steady aeroplane for formation leading', he says, 'and the combinations have been almost limitless.'

Quite a few have been de Havilland-related, that at 2008's Flying Legends showcasing the 'trilogy' of biplane twins – the DH84 Dragon, DH89A and DH90 Dragonfly. In 2011 the sky was shared with the Dragons belonging to Sir Torquil Norman and Aer Lingus. Types with royal connections were the link at the Jubilee Air Show in 2012, G-AGJG being combined with two Chipmunks (among them the very aircraft on which the now King Charles learned to fly) and an Anson. That September, it was Mark who suggested the 'Big Biplanes' combine, the Rapide, a Swordfish from the Royal Navy Historic Flight and an Antonov An-2 making their stately way along the airfield. Those are but a selection.

But beyond that, there's a wider contribution.. Several times G-AGJG has been provided to IWM for passenger

flight purposes, perhaps most memorably on the day of 2009's Autumn Air Show. There, as well as featuring in the flying programme's tribute to the Air Transport Auxiliary, Mark flew ATA veterans Molly Rose and Freydis Sharland, hosted by leading women display pilots Anna Walker and Carolyn Grace. Occasions like that, or chance encounters with museum visitors who remember Rapides – some this very specimen from its 1950s joyriding days at Heathrow, no less, with Island Air Services – are a major part of what makes it all so worthwhile.

More fundamentally, a direct thread can be followed from Mark's part in G-AGJG's restoration to the establishment of de Havilland Support. Without its role as the type certificate holder for the Tiger Moth and the Rapide, Classic Wings' pleasure flying operations would not be possible. In turn, it's allowed Mark to fly additional de Havilland types at the kind invitation of their owners, among them New Zealander Bruce Broady's beautiful Fox Moth, which he's piloted at several recent Duxford Flying Days. Unusual formations have once more been the order of the day.

After the Rapide was completed, Mark wrote of how Duxford was 'the one venue in the wide world where all this could have happened'. How true that's been for many a project during the past half-century, and counting – but its home-grown success stories don't come much more heartwarming than this.

'The greatest display act I've ever seen at Duxford was the South African Airways Boeing 747-400 display at the 2003 Centenary of Flight Air Show; even today when we talk about Duxford, my 80-year-old friend talks about that day. It was absolutely magnificent – I can even see its entrance round the back of the AirSpace hangar and the spiral climb as if it was last week. Phenomenal!'

David Marklew

YOUR MEMORIES | 2000s

'One outstanding memory of Duxford is meeting for the first time my long-lost English cousins at the steps leading up to the Concorde. Another is chatting with Elly Sallingboe, the operator of *Sally B*, the B-17 Flying Fortress, when she offered me a flight to France with them to an air show. If only I'd said yes! The hangars, the collections, the restoration halls and the air shows have provided many memories since 2000 for me. Flying Legends was always a favourite with so many warbirds flying to an amazingly well-orchestrated flying schedule. There is nowhere else in the world like Duxford.'

Frank York, Melbourne, Australia

Clockwise from left At the 2000 Autumn Air Show, Rod Dean gave the last display of Meteor F8 VZ467, owned by Kennet Aviation, before it left Britain for Australia. © John Dunnell; Nearest the camera is the Friedkin collection's A-36A ground attack version of the P-51, which was brought over to Flying Legends 2002 and became the first Allison-engined Mustang to fly in Britain since wartime. With it is the Dutch-owned P-51D *Damn Yankee*. © Ben Dunnell; Elly Sallingboe with *Sally B* at the September 2007 display. © Mike Sampson; John Romain led this B-25 Mitchell trio during 2009's Flying Legends, not long before B-25D *Grumpy*, a former member of The Fighter Collection's fleet, left to join the Flying Heritage Collection in Seattle. The other two Mitchells were B-25Js from the Royal Netherlands Air Force Historic Flight and Christian Amara, whose P-40N Warhawk tucked in at the back. © Ben Dunnell

1903

The Mighty 747 'Jumbo'

Thanks to South African Airways, the Boeing 747 will make its Duxford air display debut at this show

During the late 1960s, some 50,000 Boeing people belonged to a group called "The Incredibles". These were the construction workers, mechanics, engineers, secretaries and administrators who made aviation history by building the boeing 747 – the largest civilian aircraft in the world – in less than 16 months.

The incentive for creating the giant 747 came from reductions in air fares, an explosion in air-passenger traffic and increasingly crowded skies. In addition, Boeing had already developed the design concepts and technology of such an airplane because the company had bid on, but lost, the contract for a gigantic military transport, the C-5A.

On April 13 1966 Pan American World Airways announced a $525 million order for 25 Boeing 747s, which effectively launched the 747 programme. Within five months, orders for the 747 reached $1.8 billion. Less than three years later, on February 9, 1969 the first 747-100 had its maiden flight.

The 747's final design was offered in three configurations: all passenger, all cargo and a convertible passenger/freighter model. The freighter and convertible models loaded 8 by 8 foot cargo containers through a huge hinged nose.

The 747 was and is truly monumental in size. The massive aircraft required construction of the 200-million-cubic-foot 747 assembly plant in Everett,

Washington, the world's largest building (by volume). The fuselage of the original 747 was 225 feet long; the tail as tall as a six-story building. Pressurised, the 747 carried a ton of air. The cargo hold had room for 3,400 pieces of baggage and could be unloaded in seven minutes. The total wing area was larger than a basketball court. Yet, the entire global navigation system weighed less than a modern laptop computer.

Pilots prepared for the 747 at Boeing training school. The experience of taxiing such a large aircraft was acquired in a contraption called "Waddell's Wagon", named after Jack Waddell, the company's chief test pilot. The pilot sat in a mock-up of the 747 flight deck built atop three-storey-high stilts on a moving truck. The pilot learned how to manoeuvre from such a height by directing the truck driver below him by radio.

The National Aeronautics and Space Administration later modified two 747-100s into Shuttle Carrier Aircraft. The next version, the 747-200, holds approximately 440 passengers and has a range of about 5,600 nautical miles. In 1990, two 747-200Bs were modified to serve as Air Force One to serve as the personal aircraft of the President of the United States.

The 747-300 has an extended upper deck and carries even more passengers than the -200. The 747-400 rolled out in 1988. Its wingspan is 212 feet, and it has 6-foot-high 'winglets' on the wing tips. The 747-400 also is produced as a freighter, as a combination

freighter and passenger model, and as a special domestic version, without the winglets, for shorter-range flights.

The longer-range 747-400 aircraft (also known as 747-400ERs), were launched in late 2000. The 747-400ER, which first flew July 31, 2002, is available in both passenger and freighter versions and has a range of 8,826 miles. It incorporates the strengthened -400 Freighter wing, strengthened body and landing gear, and an auxiliary fuel tank in the forward cargo-hold, with an option for a second tank. When the 747-400ER's full-range capability is not needed, operators can remove the tank (or tanks), freeing up additional space for cargo.

The 747-400 currently the only 747 model in production continues the 747 family legacy by integrating advanced technology into one of the world's most modern and fuel-efficient airliners. The 747 continues to be the world's fastest subsonic jetliner, cruising at Mach .85 – or 85 per cent of the speed of sound. With the lowest operating cost per ton-mile in the industry, the new-technology Boeing 747-400 Freighter is the all-cargo transport member of the 747-400 family. It can carry twice as much cargo, twice as far, as the competitor's leading freighter. Along with earlier versions, 747 Freighters – about 225 in all – carry half of all the world's freighter air cargo. Among the companies who have operated the 747 are South African Airways, Virgin Atlantic, British Airways, Pan Am, Japan Air Lines, KLM, Lufthansa, Nippon Cargo, World Airways, Martinair, Air Canada, Swissair, Sabena Northwest, Cargolux, Qantas and Air France.

747 Facts

- A 747-400 has six million parts, half of which are fasteners, as well as 171 miles (274 km) of wiring and 5 miles (8 km) of tubing.

- The 747-400 wing measures 5,600 square feet (524.9 sq m), an area large enough to hold 45 medium-sized cars.

- The 747-400 tail height is 63 feet 8 inches (19.4 m), equivalent to a six-storey building.

- The 747-400 wing weighs 95,000 pounds (43,090 kg), more than 30 times the weight of the first Boeing aircraft, the 1916 B&W.

- The 747 fleet has logged more than 35 billion statute miles (56 billion km) – enough to make 74,000 trips to the moon and back.

- The 747 fleet has flown 3.6 billion people – the equivalent of more than half of the world's population.

- A 747-400 typically takes off at 180 mph (290 km/h), cruises at 565 mph (910 km/h) and lands at 160 mph (260 km/h).

- For a typical international flight, one 747 operator uses about 5.5 tons (5,000 kg) of food supplies and more than 50,000 in-flight service items.

- Engine noise from today's 747-400 is half of what it was on the original 747s delivered in 1970.

- The 747-400 can carry more than 57,000 gallons of fuel (215,745 L).

- A 747-400 that flies 3,500 statute miles (5,630 km) and carries 126,000 pounds (56,700 kg) of fuel will consume an average of five gallons (19 L) per mile.

- The 747-400 carries 3,300 gallons (12,490 L) of fuel in the horizontal (tail) stabilizer, allowing it to fly an additional 400 miles.

- At 31,285 cubic feet (876 m³), the 747-400 has the largest passenger interior volume of any commercial airliner, which is equivalent to more than three houses each measuring 1,500 square feet (135 m²).

- The Wright brothers' first flight at Kitty Hawk could have been performed within the 150-foot (45 m) economy section of a 747-400.

1903

The Royal Air Force Red Arrows

2003 is the Red Arrows' 39th display season and the second season with Squadron Leader Carl 'Spike' Jepson as Officer Commanding and Team Leader. The Team is keen to build on the success of last season's display and continue to strive to set the benchmark in formation aerobatic display flying. The Royal Air Force Aerobatic Team has a rich history and it follows in the footsteps of a list of distinguished aviators who have so successfully represented the highest standards and traditions of the Royal Air Force.

In this centenary year of powered flight, the Royal Air Force Aerobatic Team is proud to acknowledge the contribution made by the early pioneers who demonstrated the desire, bravery and commitment in pushing the known limits and boundaries of flight.

All members of the Team have worked extremely hard over the winter training season to prepare a display that conforms to the high standards expected of the Royal Air Force. The achievement of this goal has depended on the excellent training received within the Royal Air Force and on the personal qualities which are the foundations on which the Service is built – motivation, professionalism, self-discipline and teamwork.

The Squadron consists of almost 100 men and women from all walks of life who represent a broad cross-section of the trades available in the Service. The professional training they receive is second-to-none and they confidently undertake complex tasks in order to routinely deliver 9 Hawk aircraft to the team on time, every time.

The Pilots

Since mid-1966 there have been nine Red Arrows display pilots each year, including the Team Leader. All Red Arrows pilots are volunteers. To be eligible to apply for the Team, pilots must have completed at least one operational tour on a front line fast jet such as the Tornado, Harrier and Jaguar, and have a minimum of 1,500 flying hours. Pilots must also have been assessed in their annual reports as being above average in their operational role. These provisos mean that the volunteers are usually Flight Lieutenants in their late twenties or early thirties. Each display pilot stays with the Team for a three-year tour of duty. The reason for this is that by changing three pilots each year the experience level within the Team is optimised. At the end of their tour of duty with the Red Arrows, pilots usually return to "front-line" RAF squadrons. Each year, around thirty pilots apply for the Team. A short list of nine spend a week with the Red Arrows, and are put though a rigorous programme of interviews, flying tests and assessments of their personal qualities and motivation. It is vitally important that all the Red Arrows' display pilots not only trust each other's skills but get on well together. The current pilots make their final choices at a closed meeting chaired by the Commandant of the Central Flying School (CFS).

If one of the pilots goes sick during the display season, or for any other reason is not able to fly, the Team is able to fly an 8-ship formation. There are no reserve pilots for safety reasons; one spare pilot could not possibly learn all nine positions to the standard required. The pilots always fly in the same position within the formation and it takes an intensive six-month training programme for each pilot to become thoroughly proficient at flying in his position.

In addition to the nine display pilots, another pilot known as 'Red 10', the Team's Road Manager, flies another Hawk aircraft. This is sometimes called to act as a spare aircraft in the case of an engineering problem while the Team is away from base.

The BAE SYSTEMS Hawk

Since entering service with the Royal Air Force in 1976, the Hawk has established an unrivalled reputation as a fast jet trainer and its success is reflected in sales to 18 customers worldwide. Most recently, Canada and South Africa selected Hawk to meet the fighter trainer requirements of their respective armed forces. Hawk operates in extreme environments that range from Finland in the Arctic Circle to Saudi Arabia in the arid Middle East and Malaysia in the Tropics. By any standard the Hawk is the world's most successful fast jet trainer. From every standpoint it outclasses the opposition.

Reds 2003

The Red Arrows' Aircraft

The Red Arrows operate 12 Hawk 1/1a aircraft, as follows:

XX227 – Founder aircraft (with the Team since 1980)

XX233 – Joined the Team in 1988 from 4FTS

XX237 – First used by Reds in 1985

XX253 – Founder aircraft

XX260 – Founder aircraft

XX264 – Founder aircraft

XX266 – Founder aircraft

XX292 – Joined the Team in 1996 from 4FTS

XX294 – Joined the Team in 1988 from 4FTS

XX306 – Founder aircraft

XX307 – Joined the Team in 1996 from HQ CFS

XX308 – Joined the Team in 1985

The 2003 team are:

Red One – Sqn Ldr Spike Jepson

Red Two – Flt Lt Jez Griggs

Red Three – Flt Lt Dunc Mason

Red Four – Flt Lt Dan Simmons

Red Five – Sqn Ldr John Green

Red Six – Sqn Ldr Myles Garland

Red Seven – Flt Lt David Thomas

Red Eight – Flt Lt Antony Parkinson

Red Nine – Sqn Ldr Christian Gleave

Red Ten – Flt Lt Steve Underwood

ALL PHOTOS:
E. J. VAN KONINGSVELD.

LARGE FORMATION FLYPASTS

by Rod Dean

Large formation flypasts have been a feature of IWM Duxford's air displays for many years – and given the increasing numbers of restored historic aircraft, such as Spitfires and Hurricanes, they look likely to continue.

But putting together upwards of 30 aircraft, with various different characteristics, in the air and in formation is not the easiest of tasks, particularly in a civilian environment where the opportunity to practice is unlikely, and questions of pilot training, currency and suitability need to be addressed.

So how does Duxford go about putting together these major formations? And how do we get aircraft safely airborne and back on the ground in one piece? Well, there are certain rules to follow, some of which are fairly obvious – for instance, do all the pilots have an appropriate display authorisation? Other factors are little more obscure, such as the power differences between aircraft. For instance, early Spitfires are a lot less powerful than later models, and it's therefore unwise to put higher-powered

aircraft at the front of a formation in case lower-powered aircraft are unable to keep up. This is why the September Battle of Britain formation is led by the IWM Spitfire.

Beyond considering the engine power of the relative aircraft, the first requirement is deciding on the formation leader, who needs to be highly experienced and undoubtedly capable of pulling all the facets together and have the confidence of all the formation members in his or her ability. As the air shows take place in a civilian environment, each formation member has the right to say 'no thanks' if they are not completely happy with the plan. The same, of course, also exists on the part of the leader, who needs to be confident that all the participants will be able to cope with the final plan. As you can see, a plan is essential!

This page Brian Smith's choreography of the Battle of Britain 75th anniversary finale in 2015 brought the 17-ship of Spitfires and Seafires back across the airfield diagonally. © John Dunnell

The Plan

It is important that the 'KISS' principle – 'Keep It Simple, Stupid' – is uppermost in the leader's mind, otherwise unwanted complexity could jeopardise the safety of the flypast by pushing it beyond the capabilities of the participants. Consequently, before the final plan can be arrived at, the leader will need to consider factors such as:

— How many aircraft are we likely to have on the day?
— What are the types – and their varied characteristics such as cruise speed – that are going to be involved?
— What are the experience levels, and display qualifications, of the pilots involved? This could well dictate what can be done with the formation.
— Is there something we are trying to reflect – a specific anniversary for example – or is the formation just the finale to the overall display?

The second most important principle is flexibility. There is no point having a plan that requires exactly 16 aircraft or perfect weather if it cannot be executed under other circumstances. Life is rarely that simple, especially when working with historic aircraft and the UK weather comes into play. 'No plan survives contact with the enemy' is a frequently quoted maxim of war, and it is equally apt when leading large (or small) formations, so flexibility is our keynote.

The Briefing

Once the leader has drawn up the plan, they need to explain it clearly to all the participants. It is normal these days for the leader to circulate the plan to formation members well in advance of the flypast so any comments can be considered and dealt with before the formal briefing. The importance of the brief on the day cannot be over-emphasised and it is usually split into the following discrete sections:

— Formation composition – who goes where and in which aircraft. This is usually covered by a clear diagram, but I did know one RAF Wing Commander who also used to put the seats in the briefing room in the formation layout!
— Administrative details – radio frequencies, fuel calls etc.
— Start, taxi and take-off plan.
— The post-take-off join-up.
— The detail of the actual flypasts – heights, speeds and any formation changes between flypasts.
— The recovery plan – how we *safely* get this mass of aircraft back down on the ground with everyone in one piece.
— Emergencies and an alternative plan for bad weather, etc.

The final part of the ground activity is the 'walk-through', when immediately prior to the start-up, the whole formation walks through the plan on the ground in the formation positions they will be flying. To the crowd, this might look like something of a childish activity, but it is an essential final reminder of the plan – and it is mandatory for all formations, large or small, at Duxford.

The Flypasts

Providing the plan is straightforward, has been properly briefed and the weather is kind, then this might be the simplest part

– but it's not always so. The aim is to position the formation at around 800 to 1,000 feet over the airfield at Duxford at the right time, in the right place, and at the right speed. How this is achieved comes down to the leader and the inherent simplicity of the plan. There was one glorious occasion some years back, in the early days of these large formations, when after a request from someone in the back of the formation for a slightly slower speed, the leader – who will remain nameless – in response instantly chopped ten knots off his speed when they were about five miles out from the airfield. The concertina effect was immediate; I was leading a four-aircraft Mustang sub-formation and found myself in very close proximity to the section ahead, so the only place to go was away in a safe direction, and just about the whole formation disintegrated, albeit safely!

The Landing

This can be the really difficult bit. Duxford is fortunate in having two runways: the hard and the parallel grass runway, with the whole width of the grass usable. It allows for simultaneous stream landings on both runways and eases the problems. Ideally, the spacing between aircraft should preclude aircraft having to do long, straight-in approaches, which are not comfortable to do in Spitfires or Hurricanes given the limited forward visibility on the final approach path. The only way to achieve this is to have adequate separation between each element of four or five aircraft as they break for landing but, inevitably, there's always the likelihood of aircraft flying further and further out from the airfield, especially when avoiding overflying Duxford village. It is very important to brief how aircraft are to be separated on landing and make clear the need for all of them to roll to the end of the runway – no stopping half-way down the runway when there are 20 aircraft landing behind you! If an aircraft doesn't land and has to go round again, the procedure is to direct it to the north until everyone else is down; it is essential to fully cover this point in the brief.

The Debrief

It is important to learn the lessons from the flight, particularly on the first day of a two-day event to ensure the next day is better. Gathering all the pilots together and listening to their comments is key, and the leader may well make further adjustments to the plan for the following day based on their feedback. We must keep everyone happy and, most critically, safe.

I have been fortunate to lead some interesting formations such as the Spitfire Diamond 16 in 1998, and the crowd overflight of 19 Spitfires and Hurricanes – the 'Duxford Big Wing' – in 2000, as well as being a participant in many more of the famed Duxford 'Balbos'. Overall, the big formations can be demanding on all concerned, but when properly led can be a resounding success and add tremendously to the success of the display, so long may they continue.

Below The lead section of May 1998's big Spitfire formation, marking 60 years since the type entered service at Duxford, gets ready to roll off the grass. The author, Rod Dean, is furthest from the camera in the Historic Aircraft Collection's TE566. © John Dunnell

IWM IMPERIAL WAR MUSEUMS

DUXFORD

DUXFORD

Summe

AIR SHOW

Saturday 18 & Sunday 19 June

RD

• THE Y

• T

• KIDS' CO

• DU

DUXFORD'S GOLDEN MOMENTS: 2010–2022

The start of the 2010 season was slightly disrupted by a volcanic ash cloud from Iceland, which affected the involvement of some RAF aircraft, but the Spring Air Show still went ahead to launch the year's Battle of Britain 70th anniversary commemorations.

A new shape in the skies at Flying Legends was Thomas Jülch's Polikarpov I-16 fighter, flown in stunning fashion on the second day by Lithuanian aerobatic pilot Jurgis Kairys. The September Battle of Britain Air Show included spectacular formations of sixteen Spitfires and four Hurricanes, which took in several rare examples such as all five UK-based airworthy two-seat Spitfires. Duxford's biggest ever two-day crowd also enjoyed two national jet display teams, the Red Arrows and Patrouille de France. Assuming centre-stage at the Autumn Air Show was B-17 *Sally B* on her 65th birthday.

2011 dawned with a new theme for the Spring Air Show: 100 years of women in aviation. The Flying Bulls' Salzburg-based P-38L Lightning gave its first British displays at Flying Legends, where another high point was a four-ship of beautiful Hawker biplanes, comprising two Nimrods, a Demon and Hind. A mid-air collision near the end of Sunday's programme between a P-51 Mustang and a Skyraider thankfully caused no injuries, Mustang pilot Rob Davies bailing out, while the Skyraider landed safely. September's Duxford Air Show was notable for the last UK display from the USAF F-15E Strike Eagle Demonstration Team. While the Autumn Air Show commemorated the Korean War, a highlight was the Belgian F-16 demonstration involving flare-firing – one of Duxford's most spectacular solo routines ever.

2012 brought the Queen's Diamond Jubilee, and the Jubilee Air Show in May saw a host of aircraft with Royal connections take to the skies, as well as the first (and last) appearance on the British mainland of the French Air Force Cartouche Doré team of Epsilon training aircraft. Flying Legends

Right Crowds watching the spectacles on offer at the Duxford Air Show in September 2016. © IWM DUX 002201

opened with all three airworthy Spitfire Ias displaying together, and featured the debut of The Fighter Collection's (TFC) 'razorback' P-47G Thunderbolt *Snafu*, while the Duxford Air Show was privileged to be one of very few occasions where The Vintage Aviator's reproductions of an RE8 and Albatros D.Va for the RAF Museum flew before these First World War types were grounded for static exhibition. The Autumn Air Show was the venue for the last solo display of an RAF Hawk T1.

The Spring Air Show in **2013** saluted the 78th Fighter Group of the US Eighth Air Force, which had made its home at RAF Duxford 70 years earlier. Before the flying began, veteran ace Col. 'Bud' Anderson was taken for a flight in TFC's Mustang *Miss Velma*. An exclusive 'Eagle Squadron' of Hurricane X, Spitfire Ia, P-47G Thunderbolt and P-51C Mustang told the tale of American pilots before and after the US officially entered the war. A baking Flying Legends show included a unique formation of Gloster Gladiators, TFC's example displaying for the first time alongside Shuttleworth's. The British Airways Cargo Boeing 747-8F cast a considerable shadow over the Duxford Air Show as the largest aircraft ever to appear at the venue. The Autumn Air Show's celebration of 40 years since the first Duxford air show nearly succumbed to the weather, but it abated just in time. The Shuttleworth Miles Magister, a

participant in October 1973, was able to fly.

2014 began with another D-Day Anniversary Air Show – it brought together the largest number of invasion-striped aircraft for the 70th anniversary, including four C-47s that all served in 1944, with two arriving from the US. Other highlights were a mass of gliders and a BBMF Spitfire/RAF Typhoon duo. Just for Flying Legends, the aircraft of Fame museum's Boeing P-26 'Peashooter' was shipped over from California for the American fighter's first UK appearance. In September, the sight of two Lancasters, the BBMF's familiar example accompanied by the Canadian Warplane Heritage Museum's machine, pulled in a full-capacity crowd to the Duxford Air Show; it also witnessed the last flying appearance of Vulcan XH558 at Duxford, the delta bomber being grounded a year later, and a superb demonstration of a Boeing 727 operated for Oil Spill Response.

The **2015** VE Day Anniversary Air Show staged a 'Salute Formation' in honour of the Victory in Europe theme and B-17 *Sally B*'s 40th anniversary on the display circuit. Following restoration, the Aircraft Restoration Company's Blenheim made its long-awaited return in formation with two Spitfire Ias. The Historic Aircraft Collection's Fury I was yet another debutant, paired with Shuttleworth's Gladiator; a biplane Fury hadn't been seen in an air display since before the war. Visiting from Germany, the Airbus

Group's Bf 109G-4 took its Duxford bow at Flying Legends. Opened by a Luftwaffe airfield attack and RAF 'scramble', September's Battle of Britain Anniversary Air Show saw a record breaking 17-ship massed flypast and tailchase of Spitfires and Seafires. As if that wasn't enough, the BBMF offered its own six-aircraft Hurricane and Spitfire salute.

Something of a trans-Atlantic flavour was in evidence during **2016**. The American Air Show marked the reopening earlier in the year of the American Air Museum, and gave Duxford its first look at a US Air Force CV-22B Osprey with its tilt-rotors. Then an F-22A Raptor fighter took part in the USAF Heritage Flight display alongside a P-51D at Flying Legends. 'Meet the Fighters' was the Duxford Air Show's theme, commemorating the 80th anniversaries of the Spitfire and the formation of RAF Fighter Command.

A new season-opening show arrived in **2017** with the Duxford Air Festival, where the scene-stealing French Air Force Rafale made its Duxford debut, alongside rare visiting acts like the Noorduyn Norseman from the Norwegian Spitfire Foundation. Sadly, Naval Aviation Ltd's Sea Vixen belly-landed back at its Yeovilton base after appearing on the Saturday, making this the dramatic classic jet's final air show. Five Hurricanes were a highlight of Flying Legends, and again the Hawker fighter was given special prominence at the September show, which would now be

called the Battle of Britain Air Show every year – it featured a record-breaking six-ship opening sequence of Hurricanes, followed by a finale of five in formation with the Spitfire Ias, the Blenheim and Shuttleworth's Gladiator.

Many visiting aircraft from overseas added a cosmopolitan feel to **2018**'s Duxford Air Festival, including the 'Alpine Anteater' C-3605 target-tug from 46 Aviation in Switzerland. Flying Legends recalled the classic *Battle of Britain* film with four Buchóns, courtesy of ARC and Air Leasing. Then came the Battle of Britain Air Show, earmarked by the RAF as a key celebration of its centenary. It rounded off the RAF100 season with the year's largest flying line-up of historic RAF aircraft, the finale being the biggest modern-era Spitfire flypast with 18 examples. No fewer than 16 Tiger Moths from the Tiger Nine team formed a number '100' in the sky, while RAF support included a No. 617 Squadron tribute comprising the Lancaster, a Tornado GR4 – for the last ever time in RAF service at an air show – and an F-35B.

2019's edition of the Duxford Air Festival debuted the Bader Bus Company, a team of disabled pilots flying Piper PA-28s. Soon afterwards, Daks over Duxford commemorated the D-Day 75th anniversary with 21 C-47/DC-3 variants departing Duxford in a mass flight to Normandy on 5 June. What turned out to be the final Flying

Legends show staged at Duxford included the never-to-be-repeated spectacle of five Buchóns in formation, as well as the flying debut of the Historic Aircraft Collection's remarkable DH9. The September Battle of Britain Air Show celebrated 50 years since the release of the 1969 film *Battle of Britain*, large parts of which were filmed at Duxford, with an 'At the Movies' theme; four Buchóns, performing as Messerschmitt Bf 109s, were chased by three Spitfires and four Hurricanes. It was a fitting end to a decade of unique events, amazing crowds and special displays that continued to put Duxford at the heart of the British air show scene.

As Duxford looked ahead to an even brighter decade of displays in **2020**, all was put on hold with the arrival of the COVID-19 pandemic. Despite the cancellation of all three main air shows, IWM still managed to stage three Showcase Days.

With a later-than-usual start to the main Duxford show season in **2021**, the easing of COVID-19 restrictions finally enabled the Summer Air Show to resume in July. In tribute to the incredible work of the NHS throughout the pandemic, the NHS-marked Spitfire PRXI PL983 from the Aircraft Restoration Company performed paired aerobatics with the OFMC's MkIX MH434. The Red Arrows closed the weekend against a dramatic backdrop of thundery skies. The Battle of Britain Air Show in September presented

Britain's largest historic aircraft display since 2019, concluding with a mixed formation of eleven Spitfires and four Hurricanes.

The **2022** Summer Air Show brought a UK debut from the long-established Dutch-based Fokker Four team of S11 Instructors. September's Battle of Britain Air Show opened with a two-minute silence in honour of the late Queen Elizabeth II, followed by the spectacular arrival of John Romain in the 'NHS' Spitfire. The Czech Air Force also returned to Duxford for the first time since the Second World War, with a Mil Mi-35 and Mi-171 helicopter duo demonstration, and a solo Mi-35. Despite the challenges of the last few years, Duxford continues to create magic at its air shows, and will generate golden memories for years to come.

From top left Some superb C-47 formations graced Duxford in the 2010s. This one, at the Daks over Normandy event, mixed the UK-based Aces High aeroplane with two of the trans-Atlantic visitors, from the Tunison Foundation and the Commemorative Air Force. © Ben Dunnell; A tribute to the outstanding abilities of Guy Black and his team at Aero Vintage/Retrotec, the Airco DH9 operated by the Historic Aircraft Collection made its display debut at Flying Legends 2019 – the first genuine Second World War bomber to have taken to the air in the modern era. © Harry Measures; The BBMF and Canadian Warplane Heritage Lancasters caused the Duxford Air Show 2014 to sell out. © Ben Dunnell

A FLYING DISPLAY DIRECTOR'S RETROSPECTIVE

by Jeanne Frazer

or a flying display director in the early noughties, the glittering prize at Duxford was that in hosting several significant private collections of Second World War aircraft, the historic hangars serendipitously sheltered the largest concentration of rare, airworthy warbirds anywhere in Europe.

Tantalisingly, these mighty steeds were on call for Duxford air shows. A crucial aspect of this happy alliance was that a healthy proportion of the country's foremost display pilots volunteered their time and expertise to fly them.

That alone renders it quite a challenge to nominate a mere handful of stand-out moments, when pretty well every fabulously energetic warbird routine was impeccably delivered. Casting back over nigh on a hundred air show days across a 15-year tenure as IWM Duxford's FDD, an elaborate succession of images and memories float effortlessly into focus. The frisson of hosting the oh-so-stylish French national aerobatic team, the Patrouille de France, in 2006, and the delight of welcoming them back on a regular basis

thereafter. And in the realm of high performance military jets, it didn't get any better than the Belgian Air Component F-16, which evolved into yet another repeat visitor, as well as the first at Duxford to launch pyrotechnics to such great effect.

At the opposite end of the spectrum, one of the most satisfying and unusual items was the multiple glider launch, staged at the 2014 D-Day Anniversary Air Show in salute to the troop-carrying gliders' mission. Then there were the light aircraft aerobatic teams which never failed to make a huge impact: the cleverly-choreographed and perfectly-judged-in-every-way Aerostars, and the consistently brilliant, gravity-defying Matadors. A one-off which resonated for me was the

2010 Rothmans Aerobatic Team tribute, which saw two independent Pitts duos joining forces to perform a four-ship loop. Another strong image I treasure is of three C-47s, at the end of an exquisite formation, touching down delicately and in perfect concert on the grass; poetry in motion.

In 2003, having dreamt up the concept of presenting a hundred aircraft to commemorate the centenary of flight, it soon dawned that an innovative approach was essential if they were all to be squeezed into a finite display period. The solution was to assemble a random confection of up to eight light aircraft with similar performance, for which some creative mind coined the title 'flutter-by'. Hung as a single item under a rather flimsy connection, they were flung together in an all-too-brief slot during which each had to get airborne, find a way to be fleetingly but obviously centre stage, and land. Thanks to competent pilots with a sense of humour, these diverting little gaggles proved highly entertaining.

The centenary event certainly scored in exploring the extremes of flight, with the joyful sight of a flock of geese getting airborne from the grass to follow their ultralight mothership around the sky and, in need of a somewhat longer runway, the South African Airways Boeing 747-400 which took off from London Heathrow, to be released from the cocoon of controlled airspace six miles from Duxford. Captain Grant McAlpine then followed the visual route we had shown him earlier that week aboard a de Havilland Rapide to track behind the crowd and hangars, in readiness to bank and turn for the initial pass. Scanning north from the roof of the control tower, all I was able to glimpse of the giant airliner was its tail, progressing shark-like above the tree tops. Never had there been, or will there ever be, bigger goose-bumps. The massive beast swept in low, casting a shadow over the flightline. Forget straight and level flypasts. Elegantly flown, as if weighing nothing, this was a polished and extraordinarily agile demonstration, contained within an astonishingly tight radius and achieved with minimal noise. Following a gear-down approach to 100 feet, the 'jumbo jet' initiated a majestic spiral climb to 12,000 feet, to bid us farewell and disappear from view.

But warbirds, and Spitfires in particular, triumph as Duxford's bread-and-butter signature. The combined soundtrack and visual spectacle, as the enviable gaggle of close on 20 machines coughed and spluttered into life, waddled into take-off order on the runway and roared off into the blue was awesome, as indeed were the stream landings, waves and smiles from the cockpits as the aircraft taxied back along the crowd line, and engine shut-downs. Spitfires at Duxford to me are epitomised by the large massed formations staged over the years to commemorate a Battle of Britain anniversary, and the soul-stirring, spine-tingling sequences devised, briefed and led so calmly by Brian Smith. His flair for simple yet brilliant choreography would satisfy the demand for one or two stately formation passes before the elements separated and picked up speed to thunder across the airfield in opposition at low level in a series of exuberant and exhilarating tailchases. With the elliptical wing profiles shown off to their best in the high-wingover reverses at either end of the display line, a two or three-ship would execute tight formation loops high over centre point, as the majority roasted around at full throttle below. Spitfires captured in every imaginable angle of flight populated the sky. That the unmistakable growls of Merlins and Griffons reverberated around an airfield with real battle history, echoing off hangars where the ghosts of Bader, Deere and Malan roam, served only to swell the poignancy of such salutes to the 'Few', and to personify all that was elevating and intoxicating about Duxford.

That the unmistakable growls of Merlins and Griffons reverberated around an airfield with real battle history... served only to swell the poignancy of such salutes to the 'Few'...

Right Capping off a succession of brilliant Belgian Air Component F-16AM Fighting Falcon displays at Duxford, at the 2012 Jubilee Air Show Cdt Renaud 'Grat' Thys fired flares aplenty. © John Dunnell

'The two-minute silence for HM the Queen, followed by a wonderful solitary Spitfire tribute display, made the 2022 Battle of Britain Air Show a very special day – there was not a dry eye at Duxford.'

David Easdale

YOUR MEMORIES | 2010–2022

'I took my daughter, then aged 8, to Duxford for the first time at the 2018 RAF 100 air show. I remember her turning to me after the roaring sound of a low-flying Tornado and expressing how much she loved it. My daughter, now aged 12, was so inspired by Duxford that she has since joined the Air Cadets with a view to pursuing a career in the Royal Air Force.'

Dave Allen

Clockwise from left Recalling the *Battle of Britain* filming more potently than ever before, no less than five Buchóns flew together at Duxford's final Flying Legends in 2019. Four of them had been returned to flight by Air Leasing in less than two years; the fifth was from the Aircraft Restoration Company. © John Dunnell; The Red Arrows performing against a dramatic sky at the 2021 Summer Air Show. © IWM 2021 028 0409; Czech-manned RAF squadrons were resident at Duxford during wartime, but it took until the 2022 Battle of Britain Air Show for the modern Czech Air Force to return. It did so with two helicopters, including this spectacularly painted Mil Mi-35 attack helicopter. © IWM 2022 054 031; Hurricanes after sundown at the Battle of Britain Air Show in 2019. © IWM 2019 082 01

Commemorating
Victory

Above:
An in-cockpit view of the
1946 Victory Day flypast,
captured from within
the No. 254 Squadron
Beaufighter element.
(AEROPLANE)

The early post-war years saw many memorable aerial events being staged in honour of the Allied victory during the Second World War, some also providing a much-anticipated chance to see wartime German technology at first-hand. Ben Dunnell, this weekend's flying display commentator and the editor of *Aeroplane* magazine, looks back at some of the major occasions in 1945-46.

As IWM Duxford this weekend celebrates the 70th anniversary of VE Day, thoughts turn not only to the events that led up to the end of the Second World War, but also the way they have been marked in the past. This venue has itself, not least 10 and 20 years ago, staged major air shows with Victory in Europe anniversaries as their theme. But these are traditions that date back to the immediate post-war period, when Britain commemorated the Allied triumph with a number of impressive aerial events.

At Duxford – not then an RAF station, but US Army Air Force Station 357 – took place one of the earliest post-war air events. The Americans celebrated Air Force Day on 1 August 1945, and a number of US bases in Britain opened their doors for the occasion. For many members of the public it was a first chance to get 'up close' to Army Air Force aircraft types that had flown from these shores, and the opportunity was taken with enthusiasm. At Duxford some 5,000 people were recorded as attending. There they could inspect at very close quarters a number of the 78th Fighter

Group's P-51D and P-51K Mustangs, some with panels off. Photos also show that at least one visiting P-47 Thunderbolt and B-17 Flying Fortress were present, too.

At the time of Air Force Day the 78th Fighter Group was expecting to be transferred to the Pacific theatre, but the dropping of the atom bombs and Japan's surrender changed all that. Instead, exactly a month on from its Duxford 'open house', there came for the group news that it was to return Stateside and disband. This was, therefore, the one and only time it held a public occasion here.

Already, by then, the bombed-out site of a former John Lewis department store on London's Oxford Street had become a centre of some aeronautical attention. There from June to September 1945 were exhibited eight operational RAF and Fleet Air Arm aircraft – an Auster IV, Beaufighter TFX, Firefly I, Halifax III, Mosquito XVI, Spitfire IX, Tempest V and Walrus II – plus sections of a Lancaster and a Horsa glider, and the experimental Gloster E28/39 jet testbed. According to *The Aeroplane Spotter*, some two million people attended. Clearly there was a significant public appetite to inspect at first hand the aircraft that had won the war.

New commemorative traditions were soon established. 15 September became known as Battle of Britain Day, remembering the date in 1940 on which major Luftwaffe raids against London had failed to deliver a decisive blow, causing postponement of Germany's invasion plans. At lunchtime on 15 September 1945, the skies over London were filled with some 300 aircraft participating in the first big British military flypast of the post-war years. Heading the way were a dozen Spitfire IXs each flown by a Battle of Britain pilot, led by then-Wing Commander Douglas Bader, at the time commanding officer of the Fighter Command Sector Headquarters at North Weald. At that famous fighter base in Essex, Bader and his fellow members of 'the Few' met once again with Lord Dowding, 'boss' of Fighter Command during the Battle of Britain, prior to their departure.

Behind were some 300 more RAF aircraft, comprising Mustangs, Tempests, Typhoons, Meteors, Mosquitos and Beaufighters. They flew, according to the No. 11 Group operations record book, a route that began with a rendezvous over North Weald at 12.35hrs and saw the massive aerial parade passing overhead St Paul's Cathedral at 12.40hrs. It and ground activities in central London, including a large march-past of aviation industry workers and members of the military, formed part of the launch of Thanksgiving Week, a nationwide scheme to promote savings and investments in the name of post-war rebuilding. A message from King George VI said, *"We are now free to start on the tremendous tasks of reconstruction. I trust that the success of the Thanksgiving Week campaign will reflect the high resolution which the British people bring to the shaping of the future."*

"Two circuits over London and its environs were made" wrote *Flight* magazine's reporter, *"omitting,*

strangely enough, the south-eastern suburbs. They, surely, deserved a show more than anyone. The route was Ilford, Poplar, Hyde Park, Northolt, Northwood, Elstree, Finchley, Hackney, Deptford, Wimbledon, Deptford, Teddington, Welsh Harp, Finchley and out over Ponders End and back to North Weald." Still the damage inflicted on the capital was clear to see, but plans could now be made for a peaceful future, and in this Thanksgiving Week played its part. RAF stations also opened their doors in salute to the Battle of Britain, starting another long-standing feature of the aviation calendar. A widespread programme of so-called Battle of Britain 'At Home Days' would persist for many decades to come.

Aside from the Meteors featured in the flypast, the march of jet aircraft progress was illustrated that day by a demonstration over London of a prototype Vampire fighter, in the hands of Geoffrey de Havilland. This was an area of technology in which the Germans had achieved great things, and soon it was possible to see just how great. Part of the Thanksgiving Week activities, a small exhibition of captured German aircraft opened in Hyde Park on 16 September, but better was to come.

The Royal Aircraft Establishment at Farnborough amassed a spectacular assembly of German machines, and there they were put on display during October and November 1945, public opening taking place from 10 to 12 November. Finally, people were able to see what Britain had been up against in terms of aeronautical technology. The catalogue, today held by the National Archives, said: *"The object of this exhibition is to give the visitor a general idea of the aircraft and equipment in use with the German Air Force at the end of the war."* Even the most seasoned observers found it almost overwhelming. No wonder, when considering the presence of such German innovations as the tandem-engined Dornier Do 335A fighter, the Blohm und Voss BV 155B high-altitude interceptor, the rocket-powered Messerschmitt Me 163B Komet, and the tail-less Horten Ho IV glider.

For many members of the public it was a first chance to get 'up close' to Army Air Force aircraft types that had flown from these shores, and the opportunity was taken with enthusiasm.

Below:
Visitors to the 78th Fighter Group's open day at Duxford on 1 August 1945 climb over P-51D Mustang 44-14251 *Contrary Mary.* (National Archives and Records Administration)

Combined with the display of German types was an array of the latest British technology, such machines as the Bristol Brigand, de Havilland Dove and Hornet, Hawker Fury (not, here, in navalised Sea Fury guise), Martin-Baker MB5 and Vickers Viking being seen in public for the first time. *"Never in aviation history"*, wrote *Flight*, *"has there been such a complete and up-to-date show of aircraft and ancillaries."*

Some of the aeroplanes were demonstrated in the air, Geoffrey de Havilland taking top honours in *Flight's* view for his Vampire display. *"By contrast with the Vampire and the Meteor"*, its initial report went on, *"the two German jet aircraft"* – a Messerschmitt Me 262A-1 and Heinkel He 162A-2 being flown – *showed by how far this country had advanced. They were very fast, but at the price of fantastic stalling speeds and grimly extended take-off runs, and were a credit more to the courage of German pilots – and, incidentally, to that of the two Farnborough pilots who flew them at the display."*

The luck of one, alas, was to run out. On 9 November the He 162 was lost, together with pilot Flight Lieutenant Marks and a serviceman on the ground, when the aircraft suffered a structural failure during an aerobatic manoeuvre. Testing such machines brought potentially significant risks. However, *Flight* concluded, the Heinkel and Messerschmitt jets *"showed how near we might have been to a possible loss of air supremacy"*. It called the Farnborough event *"a monument to German ingenuity and energy, while, by its very diversity, demonstrating a state of panic at a time when they must have known that the end was near."*

The jet age was now upon us, but still piston-engined aircraft held sway when Victory Day was celebrated the following year. The date chosen was rather strange: 8 June 1946, a year and one month after VE Day itself. Again a major flypast over London was planned, naturally in meticulous detail. It was to overfly the Royal saluting base between Admiralty Arch and Buckingham Palace, and involved aircraft (front-line types only) from the RAF and Fleet Air Arm. Given the speed differentials between the different sections

Above:
78th Fighter Group P-51 Mustangs, plus a visiting P-47 Thunderbolt and, in the background, a B-17 Flying Fortress, on show at Duxford on 1 August 1945. (National Archives and Records Administration)

Right:
At RAF North Weald, Douglas Bader climbs into Spitfire IX RK917, bearing his personal 'DB' code, for the Thanksgiving Day flypast on 15 September 1945. (Via Ben Dunnell)

Below:
An impressive line-up of German 'heavies' at Farnborough – Fw200C-4/U1, Ju 352A, Ju 290A-2 and Ar 232B. (AEROPLANE)

involved, ranging from Sunderland flying boats at 130kt to Meteor and Vampire jets at somewhere in the region of 300kt, great precision was called for. *"All leaders or deputy leaders must have accurate watches with second hands"*, instructed the No. 11 Group order for the flypast. *"Commands and Groups are responsible that these be made available."*

And so it went off, despite dire weather on the day. A solitary Hurricane led the stream, even though, in *Flight's* words, *"when it came into view only a few shelterers forsook the dripping trees in Hyde Park."* Following on were Sunderlands, Halifax transports, Lancasters, Beaufighters, Firebrands, Fireflies, Seafires, Spitfires, Hornets, Tempests, Meteors and Vampires, a mixture indicative of the 'changing of the guard'. Soon, many of the propeller-driven types would be gone from service — here was a chance to salute their contribution. That the people of London, and visitors from further afield, did. Thankfully, they could see most of the formations through the murk. A *Flight* reporter aboard a Mosquito of No. 4 Squadron wrote of how, quite frequently, *"the aircraft immediately ahead — spaced only one machine's length away — would be out of sight."*

Today, quite rightly, safety considerations would preclude any flying in such awful conditions. Nearly 70 years ago, attitudes were rather different. Yet still there exists a strong desire to celebrate the Allied victory and commemorate the fallen, and IWM Duxford has several times played its part. On 8 May 1995, exactly 50 years since the German

surrender, from this airfield was mounted a historic aircraft flypast over Buckingham Palace, its departure a pre-show feature at that year's VE Day Anniversary Air Show. July 2005 saw a larger London flypast to mark the 60th anniversaries of both VE and VJ Days, the second day of the Flying Legends Air Show witnessing the launch of no fewer than 19 aircraft — five Dragon Rapides, a Lockheed 12, Catalina, two Ansons, three DC-3s/C-47s, two each of B-17 Flying Fortresses and B-25 Mitchells, and the Battle of Britain Memorial Flight's Lancaster, Hurricane and Spitfire — bound for the Palace. On a glorious summer afternoon, many memories were evoked.

This weekend's VE Day Anniversary Air Show will witness its own spectacular commemorative flypast led by B-17 Flying Fortress *Sally B*. While it may no longer be possible to muster upwards of 300 aircraft for a massed aerial parade, the spirit of those events in 1945-46 lives on.

Above:
Part of the mouthwatering array of enemy aircraft contained in the outdoor static display at RAE Farnborough in October-November 1945.
(AEROPLANE)

Left:
Some of the RAF jet fighters involved in the Victory Day flypast were Meteor IIIs of No. 245 Squadron.
(AEROPLANE)

in conversation with
JOHN ROMAIN

by Elliott Marsh

John Romain was 14 when he volunteered at Duxford's first air show in October 1973. Now Managing Director of the Aircraft Restoration Company, he's played a fundamental role in Duxford's historic aircraft preservation scene for more than four decades.

This page John Romain in the cockpit of IWM's Supermarine Spitfire Mark 1a N3200.

'Back in '73, I was sneaking away from school to volunteer with the East Anglian Aviation Society – the guy running Duxford at the time used to write us sick notes', he recalls. 'I ended up working here in the week leading up to the air show and over the air show weekend. I didn't have any money, so I'd sleep in the vehicles in the hangars. The Society's primary job was to get the hardstanding ready for the air show. We went out onto the runway with barrels of tar and watering cans, pouring tar into the gaps on this blistered and broken concrete runway. We put up wicker fencing for the crowdlines. We painted loads of 50-gallon drums red-white-red to place around the site as rubbish bins.

'I was the radio operator on the "Follow Me" Willys Jeep at the first event.

Subsequently, I volunteered my services looking after Ormond Haydon-Baillie's aeroplanes. You'd see some wild departures. One of the most impressive was a Fairey Gannet that circled back over the airfield, passing very low between two of the Belfast Truss hangars. Similarly, when they were digging up ground to lay the M11 there was a huge earthen bank to the south of the airfield – this Buccaneer came through very low and picked up over the mound. The jet efflux just blew this bank apart!'

6 May 1984 was Romain's first air show display at Duxford, piloting an Auster AOP9 alongside Lee Proudfoot in a Chipmunk. 'We were young, but we had the experienced ex-military boys here watching us, enthusiastically teaching us the way forward. 'Hoof' Proudfoot took on the role of mentor when I started flying the Harvard, with the

'The barrier line is clear, the aeroplanes are put away, everything is hushed, the air's cooling and the sun's low – and you get the feeling you're not quite on your own'.

intention of one day converting me to single-engine fighters. It was Lindsey Walton bringing his Corsair to Duxford that gave me my first step into flying heavy warbirds. Spitfire IX MH434 followed, with Ray and Mark Hanna giving me the ground briefing.'

While weekdays were dedicated to engineering and maintenance at ARC, summer weekends were spent demonstrating warbirds for the Duxford operators under the tutelage of John Larcombe, 'Hoof' Proudfoot and Mark Hanna. They were, he says, 'Some of the most generous individuals I've had the privilege of flying alongside – I owe a great deal to their patience and compassion.'

In the nineties, Romain says, 'Duxford moved towards more of an emphasis on the number of aircraft in one slot than singleton displays. It was exciting, getting airborne with

From left John Romain and Lee Proudfoot about to fly their first formation display together at Duxford. © Aircraft Restoration Company; John Romain standing by the tail of Lindsey Walton's Corsair. Thanks to Lindsey's kindness, generosity and trust in John, this was the first warbird John ever flew. © Aircraft Restoration Company; John Romain piloting the 'NHS' Spitfire after the two-minute silence in honour of the late Queen Elizabeth II at the Battle of Britain Air Show in 2022. ©Aircraft Restoration Company

six or seven fighters peeling around the sky. We started to learn how to fly large formations in multiple types of aircraft. Duxford has benefitted from having the machines and the pilots with the skills set to fly them. That's why the air shows here are so slick, and why we're able to launch those huge formations every year without rehearsing. Unthinkable back when this all started. It's a testament to the system we have in place here.'

Romain's memories of Duxford air shows are many and varied – high points include flying the Blenheim and Mosquito together at Classic Fighter 1993; arriving crowd-rear in an 18-strong Spitfire and Hurricane 'Big Wing' in September 2000; leading a three-ship B-25 Mitchell tailchase at Flying Legends 2009 and a Buchón trio at Flying Legends 2011; and participating in numerous iterations of the 'Mercury Flight', with the Blenheim joined by multiples of Lysanders and Gladiators.

Most recently, he opened Duxford's Battle of Britain Air Show 2022 flying ARC's Spitfire PRXI PL983 in tribute to Her Majesty Queen Elizabeth II. 'I'll never forget that. The weight of the occasion is certainly something you think about. I was asked to break the two minutes' silence. That added pressure, particularly given the need to get airborne and head north so people couldn't hear the Spitfire holding during the silence.

'If I was running in from 500 feet north of Duxford, it's unlikely the public would hear me, but I'd not have the energy I need for the routine. A dive in from height would mean the public would hear the Spitfire on the descent; but perhaps that's a good thing. To achieve an on-time arrival, the public will hear you running in at some point. Overthinking it tends to mean you won't achieve it and you won't enjoy it. Enjoyment – the public's and our own – is fundamentally why we fly at air shows. Never should it just be going out there to do a job.

'There's an atmosphere to this place – an awful lot of history', he says. 'Often, you'll fly at an air show and the place is full of people, buzzing all morning and afternoon. After the show, you'll sit with a beer and debrief outside the marquee as the spectators and the cars start to disperse. As the sun drops, you walk back to the hangar on the live side of the airfield. The barrier line is clear, the aeroplanes are put away, everything is hushed, the air's cooling and the sun's low – and you get the feeling you're not quite on your own. There's something reassuring in that.'

AERIAL / COLLECTIVE
D U X F O R D

A PLACE I KNOW

Among the clouds is a place I know

Free from the burdens far down below

And I've witnessed a steed that can carry you there

So you too may gallop through pastures of air

You see -

This place,

Only the winged may chance;

The great halls of sky in which they dance

Beyond the horizon -

Look!

Just there!

A place I know - the Spitfire's lair...

by Aerial Collective.

Our guests are often surprised by the level of emotion that ensues from their day with Aerial Collective at Duxford. The astonishing views from the cockpit together with the weightlessness of flight inspire a sense of freedom and curiosity which many remark on as not having felt since childhood. There are those who laugh, and those who cry; those who return home with a tale to tell, and those whose smile says everything they need you to know. Whether as a lover of history, or a lover of adventure; an explorer or a dreamer. We look forward to welcoming you to Aerial Collective Duxford, and taking you on an journey...

to a place we know.

TO FIND OUT MORE
AERIALCOLLECTIVE.CO.UK
+44 (0) 1223 653 830

IMMERSIVE WARBIRD FLIGHT EXPERIENCES FROM DUXFORD AIRFIELD

DUXFORD
BATTLE
OF BRITAIN
AIR SHOW

Kids go free

Saturday 16 & Sunday 17 September 2023

Tickets selling fast!
Book now at
IWM.ORG.UK/AIRSHOWS

DUXFORD AIR SHOWS **50**

IWM shops offer a collection of products that are inspired by the stories of people whose lives have been impacted by war and conflict.

This air show weekend, browse our exclusive Duxford Air Shows 50 range in the IWM Shop located in the visitor centre and our official IWM Shop marquees.

Join us for fun activities and pop ups from:

➤ Chiltern Brewery
➤ Classic Racing Spirit
➤ Bravo Delta

IWM is a charity. Every purchase you make supports the work we do. Take home more stories at **shop.iwm.org.uk**

Retold

Every purchase helps their stories to be **retold**

DUXFORD

FLYING
FINALE

Saturday 14 October 2023

Tickets selling fast! Book now
IWM.ORG.UK/AIRSHOWS

DUXFORD 50
AIR SHOWS